Catholicism, Evolution,
And
Secular Theology

By
Thomas L. McFadden

Institute for Science and Catholicism

ISC is a non-stock Virginia corporation recognized by the IRS as a charity. ISC is promoting the renewal of a Catholic theology of creation and a new science/faith synthesis based on sound scientific data and a serious approach to the Holy Scriptures in accordance with longstanding Church Tradition.

Email: SCIENCEandCATHOLICISM@GMAIL.COM

On the web: scienceandcatholicism.org

On Facebook: Institute for Science and Catholicism

Contents

"When men cease to believe in God, they do not then believe in nothing, they believe in anything."

G. K. Chesterton (1874-1936), writer, philosopher

"Another curious aspect of the theory of evolution is that everybody thinks he understands it."

Jacques Monod (1910-1976), biochemist, 1965 Nobel Prize for Physiology or Medicine

"Theistic evolutionists are deluded."

Richard Dawkins, best-selling atheist author

"To say that animals evolved into man is like saying that Carrara marble evolved into Michelangelo's *David*."

Tom Wolfe, best-selling novelist

"Ever since the creation of the world His eternal power and divine nature, invisible though they are, have been understood and seen through the things He has made. So they are without excuse."

***Romans* 1:20**

"Catechesis on creation is of major importance. It concerns the very foundations of human and Christian life: for it makes explicit the response of the Christian faith to the basic question that men of all times have asked themselves: "Where do we come from?" "Where are we going?" "What is our origin?" "What is our end?" "Where does everything that exists come from and where is it going?" The two questions, the first about the origin and the second about the end, are inseparable. They are decisive for the meaning and orientation of our life and actions."

Catechism of the Catholic Church, paragraph 282

Preface

The accelerating loss of faith by Catholic youth is reported in survey after survey. An estimated 20 million Americans have left the Catholic Church since 2000. Today roughly 50% of American adults under 30 do not believe in Christianity's God. Once society chooses to reject God's existence, that society begins to hate the people of God. That has frightening social and political consequences as well as spiritual consequences.

Bishop Robert Barron was Chairman of the Bishops' Committee on Evangelization and Catechesis. At the U.S. Bishops' Conference meeting in June 2019, he spoke of the massive apostasy of Catholic youth and cited statistics such as "half the kids we baptized and confirmed in the last 30 years are now ex-Catholics or unaffiliated." To put that into perspective, he said that "one out of six millennials in the U.S. is now a former Catholic." He claimed that they simply no longer believe the Church's teachings and called that "the bitter fruit of the dumbing down of our faith" as it has been presented in catechesis and apologetics.

Why Catholic Catechesis Continues to Fail

The hypothesis of this book is that the "mainstream diocesan-approved" catechesis continues to fail because it inadequately answers the basic question that men of all times have asked themselves: "Where do we come from?" "Where are we going?" "What are our origins?" "What is our end?" "Where does everything that exists come from and where is it going?" According to paragraph 282 of *The Catechism of the Catholic Church,* "the first two questions, the first about the origin and the second about the end are inseparable." They "are decisive for the meaning and orientation of our life and actions."

A New Paradigm for Reading the Bible

For centuries Catholics found the answers to those questions in the first chapters of *Genesis*, the first book of the Bible. But Catholic education now looks elsewhere. Although Catholic doctrine never changed, beginning in the early 20th Century Catholic institutions and centers of formation adopted a new paradigm for reading the Bible. The late Pope Benedict XVI, when he was Prefect of the Congregation for the Doctrine of the Faith, delivered a lecture about that destructive paradigm at St. Peter's Church in New York on January 27, 1988. The title was "Biblical Interpretation in Crisis: On the Question of the Foundations and Approaches of Exegesis Today." He explained what happened to our faith in the Bible because of the new model for reading it through the lens of "science:"

> ... in the history-of-religions school, the model of evolution was applied to the analysis of biblical texts. This was an effort to bring the methods and models of the natural sciences to bear on the study of history. [Rudolf] Bultmann laid hold of this notion in a more general way and thus attributed to the so-called scientific worldview a kind of dogmatic character. Thus, for example, for him the non-historicity of the miracle stories was no question whatever anymore. The only thing one needed to do yet was to explain how these miracle stories came about... To that extent there lies in modern exegesis a reduction of history into philosophy, a revision of history by means of philosophy.

Rudolf Bultmann's Disciples

The reduction of history by philosophy, that is, the "scientific method" of exegesis that Cardinal Ratzinger criticized has been in vogue among seminary Scripture professors for at least 75 years and continues today. A good example is provided by the career of the late Fr. Bruce Vawter, a Vincentian.

Fr. Vawter was a witness for the plaintiffs who were suing the Arkansas Board of Education in 1981 because they objected to a law passed by the Arkansas Legislature which required the teaching of Creation Science along with Evolution Science in the public schools of Arkansas. From a deposition conducted by the plaintiff's law firm, one learns that Fr. Vawter was taught evolutionary biology and the evolutionary explanation of origins at the St. Thomas Seminary in Denver. When asked if there was any other approach to origins discussed in the classroom besides the evolution approach, he said that there was no conflict in the minds of the people there in "thinking about evolutionary background to the origin of this all and religion." He elaborated:

> I don't think there was any feeling on the part of anybody that there was any incompatibility in presenting it in an evolutionary structure, and at the same time, conceding that the whole thing is not by random decision, but it was a guided or a designed thing, and, therefore, it would not be a question of another model, but rather, evolution would be considered more of the process by which this came to be which would not conflict with the fact it came to be at the behest of a creator.

Fr. Vawter, at the time he gave this deposition, was a Professor and the Chairman of the Department of Religious Studies at DePaul University. His specialty was Old Testament.

In his deposition Fr. Vawter named numerous academic associations to which he belonged and said that their common denominator was the scientific study of religion just by utilizing the scientific method of biblical exegesis (explanation or interpretation of a Bible text). In other words, he was of the

3

Rudolf Bultman school. When asked to name the particular authorities he relied upon in discussing *Genesis* I and II, he replied "all of my predecessors and all the commentators and the accumulated wisdom... that's been amassed in the last couple hundred years in the scientific study of the scriptures." Fr. Vawter spent most of the years of his priesthood until his death in 1986 teaching evolution-polluted Biblical interpretation at various colleges and seminaries.

Fr. Vawter's history gives a glimpse into the academic world of professional, scholar-priests that is typical of the one in which many of our priests and bishops have been educated. Fr. Vawter was not singled out because he was unique but, rather, because he was typical, and many of today's priests and bishops have been educated by similar scholars. For example, in July 2017 a pastor in the Diocese of Arlington, Virginia wrote this in *The Catholic Thing* blog:

> In the 1980s, I attended a Midwest seminary that was schizophrenic with respect to the Faith. ... Scripture studies were essentially liberal Protestant. ... One of the Scripture professors, Father Otto, was ... a disciple of Rudolf Bultmann, the famous (or, as I prefer, the infamous) liberal Protestant theologian whose scholarly technique of "demythologizing" Scriptures corrupted generations of students. Since our Scripture studies were essentially divorced from the Catholic faith, it was only natural that we allowed Protestant seminarians to attend classes.

Another "Corrupted Generation"

In 2019, Steven C. Smith became an Associate Professor of Biblical Exegesis at the seminary known as St. Mary of the Lake, Mundelein, Il. Previously Professor Smith had been an Associate Professor of Sacred Scripture since 2008 at Mt. St. Mary's

Seminary in Maryland. Based on his biography online it seems clear that he is very intelligent and sincere. But based on his journey from Catholicism to Protestantism and back again he may have missed something regarding our Tradition. He left Catholicism as a young adult. In 2000 while earning an M.A. in New Testament Theology at Protestant Wheaton College Graduate School he re-discovered his Catholic faith. He earned his Ph. D. in New Testament & Early Christianity in 2008 at Loyola of Chicago, a Jesuit university. His doctoral dissertation was "The Determination of Criteria as Verification and Falsification Controls in the Analysis of Textual Parallels from the Jewish Wisdom Tradition and the Fourth Gospel." One can't judge a book by its cover or a dissertation by its title but that title strongly signals the historical-critical method, a.k.a, "the scientific method." "Criteria" and "Textual Analysis" are hallmarks of that method.

It Depends on How You Look at It

Based on a lecture Dr. Smith gave on October 6, 2015 in the Diocese of Arlington Virginia concerning *Genesis* 1-2 that was videoed and published by the Institute of Catholic Culture, it is easy to understand why some priests are not well prepared at the seminary to defend the Bible against the claims of evolution-based science that are peeling away our youth. Those leaving the Church perhaps agree with ex-Catholic celebrity Bill Maher that the Bible is a bunch of "silly stories."

Dr. Smith started his lecture with a story about his daughter being fitted for eye glasses and the way the eye doctor kept shifting the trial lenses in order to find the correct one to prescribe for her. From there he said that people get "tripped up because they don't have the right lenses on to see what God is saying." In order to understand *Genesis* 1-2 one has to see them through the correct "lenses." According to Smith there are three lenses through

5

which people read *Genesis* 1-2: purely scientific excluding faith, literalistic which looks at Genesis with faith but not necessarily in a reasoned way and symbolically which is the correct way (according to him it seems.) "So my hope for us tonight is to make sure we have the right lenses on as we are reading Genesis 1 and 2. Sound good?"

He then lectured from a paper he had authored and handed out called "The Liturgy of Creation: Reading Genesis 1-2 with the Wisdom of the Church." It is not obvious how "the Wisdom of the Church" was involved because his opinions were supported by 19 footnotes, none of which were "of the Church" except for #17 which was an inconsequential reference to the Catechism of the Catholic Church: "As the Catechism reminds us, the Sabbath is the heart of Israel's law." One would think that any lecture about how to read and interpret *Genesis* 1-2 might mention *Providentissimus Deus*, the definitive encyclical "On the Study of Holy Scripture" or *Dei Verbum*, the "Dogmatic Constitution on Divine Revelation."

At one point in his lecture Smith explained his intellectual triumph over any of the seminarians subject to his authority who might have become 6-day fiat creationists as the result of their parents teaching:

> Now hear this, this really startles my seminarians when I read this next quote, 'cause for them it is pulling the rug out from under the six days of creation. Listen to this very interesting quote.

The text of Genesis from 1:1 to 2:3 was presented in his paper as symbolism concerning Worshipping God in His Holy Temple, The Sacred Space of the Garden of Eden, The God of the Mountain, The Temple of Mt. Eden, and The Threefold Structure of the Cosmic Temple. The last 6 pages of the paper are a mish-

6

mash of symbolism about Temples real and spiritual and the Hebrew Sabbath. I could not detect within those pages the doctrines that the Church teaches and that are derived directly from *Genesis* 1 and 2. Dr. Smith's discussion of *Genesis* 1 and 2, particularly with its emphasis on temple symbolism has a strong resemblance to the scholarship of J.H. Walton, a well-published Protestant author and Professor of Old Testament, who joined the faculty of liberal Protestant Wheaton College around the time Smith studied there. For example, Walton's books such as *Genesis 1 As Ancient Cosmology*, *Ancient Near Eastern Thought and the Old Testament*, and *The Lost World of Genesis 1: Ancient Cosmology and the Origins Debate* are heavy on creation cosmology according to ancient Egyptian and Mesopotamian thought. Walton has written that "creation texts do follow the model of temple-building texts" For example in *Genesis 1 As Ancient Cosmology* Walton uses terms such as "close association between temple and cosmos", the "seven-day temple inauguration" and the "intrinsic relation between cosmos and temple."

Whatever one may think of Dr. Smith's paper, "The Liturgy of Creation: Reading Genesis 1-2 with the Wisdom of the Church," it must be asked if his paper owes more to the wisdom of his Protestant colleague J.H. Walton than to the wisdom of our Catholic Tradition.

The Catechism Approves of the New Paradigm

Proof that a new paradigm exists within Catholic circles for answering the questions that "are decisive for the meaning and orientation of our life and actions" is in the *Catechism* itself. To answer the questions that paragraph 282 says all men have about their origins the faithful are not referred to *Genesis* but to science:

7

283 The question about the origins of the world and of man has been the object of many scientific studies which have splendidly enriched our knowledge of the age and dimensions of the cosmos *[the big bang theory]*, the development of life forms *[abiogenesis theory]* and the appearance of man *[biological evolution from a common ancestor, i.e., Darwinism]*. These discoveries invite us to greater admiration for the greatness of the Creator, prompting us to give him thanks for all his works and for the understanding and wisdom he gives to scholars and researchers.

In other words, science explains what, when and how it happened but just remember that whatever happened, "God did it."

Truth Matters!

What if the big bang, abiogenesis, and Darwinism are not scientific facts but rather hypotheses, having some sort of scientific foundation? What if they are just attempts to explain origins from a purely materialistic viewpoint? Materialism is a philosophy. That is what Cardinal Ratzinger meant when he said that modern biblical interpretation is "a reduction of history into philosophy, a revision of history by means of philosophy."

The 1994 *Catechism*'s collaborators who blessed the evolutionary interpretation of our origins appear to have been the spiritual successors of those to whom Pope Pius XII referred in his 1950 encyclical *The Human Race: Some False Opinions Which Threaten to Undermine Catholic Doctrine (Humani Generis)*:

> In fact, not a few insistently demand that the Catholic religion take these sciences into account as much as possible. This certainly would be praiseworthy in the case

of clearly proved facts; but caution must be used when there is rather question of hypotheses, having some sort of scientific foundation, in which the doctrine contained in Sacred Scripture or in Tradition is involved. If such conjectural opinions are directly or indirectly opposed to the doctrine revealed by God, then the demand that they be recognized can in no way be admitted.

Belief in Evolution is Mainstream Catechesis

The origin of the world and of man and of all living things (with some sort of divine assistance) through hundreds of millions of years of the same kinds of material processes going on now is "mainstream Catholic catechesis" taught to most students as a scientific fact in most Catholic institutions and by the culture at-large. Many who accept that belief likewise logically conclude that no God is necessary. World-famous evolutionary biologist Richard Dawkins said it best: "Darwin made it possible to be an intellectually fulfilled atheist." Once-popular TV "Science Guy," Bill Nye in his book, *Undeniable and the Science of Creation*, said "Perhaps there is intelligence in charge of the universe, but Darwin's theory shows no sign of it and has no need of it." Writing in his 2021 book, *The Return of the God Hypothesis,* Stephen Meyer observed that

> The idea that science has buried God is pervasive in the media, in educational settings, and in culture broadly.

The Church teaches dogmatically that God is the Author of the Bible and that it is inerrant. But if *Genesis* is not the historical narrative that it seems to be, what is it? According to Bishop Barron it is "theology, mysticism, spirituality; a theological reflection on the origin of all things." What if other "miracle stories" in the Bible are no more than that? For the truth, must

9

Catholics rely on "the understanding and wisdom he gives to scholars and researchers?"

Pew Research Center and the Center for Applied Research in the Apostolate have found that most Americans have accepted that our origins, with or without divine intervention, are in cosmic and biological evolution. When they asked those who left the Church why they left, many said it was because of the disconnect between religion and science. The disconnect is that the Bible cannot be true because its account of our origins in fiat creation over 6 days clashes with our origins in cosmic and biological evolution over untold eons. Both of those conflicting accounts of origins are matters of faith, that is, matters that can neither be proved nor disproved beyond a reasonable doubt. But, to the extent that people are taught to believe on the "authority of science," that evolutionary origins are facts, it has the practical effect of disproving the *Genesis* account.

It is not the operational science and engineering that produce the goods and services we enjoy today that causes the disconnect between religion and science. The disconnect is because proponents of evolutionary origins have succeeded in conflating operational science with that oxymoron "historical science." That includes investigation of pre-historic artifacts in paleontology, anthropology, archeology, and theoretical physics. Those disciplines make careful observation of data and draw conclusions based on interpretation of the data according to the materialistic models currently in vogue.

What this Book Does

This book is limited to discussion of what the *Catechism* claims are the "many scientific studies which have splendidly enriched our knowledge of the age and dimensions of the cosmos, the development of life forms and the appearance of man" to see what evidence they have produced and if they have in fact invited "us to greater admiration for the greatness of the Creator, prompting us to give him thanks for all his works and for the understanding and wisdom he gives to scholars and researchers."

The fundamental purpose of the book then is just to provoke a reexamination within Catholic intellectual circles concerning the claims of science which have diminished faith in the Bible and caused not a few to lose faith in God as He has revealed Himself to us. Our origins can never be proved but rationale people can decide which account is most plausible if they have the relevant facts. In scientific terms that means "the inference to the best interpretation." The Bible's account of origins in Genesis is short and simple. The alternative is long and complicated. Those complications ought to be understood before one decides which explanation is more plausible.

Chapter One describes the extent to which the "scientific studies" have shaped belief. Chapter Two explains the state of evolutionary cosmology. Chapters Three and Four consider what science claims about the development of life forms and the appearance of man. Chapter Five explains evolutionary geology, the sister science of evolutionary cosmology and evolutionary biology. It proposes geological evidence for the ages of time (known as "deep time") that the other two theories depend upon.

Chapter Six explains the essential connection between evolutionary theory and the religious atheism or wokeism that drives post-Christian politics and culture. Evolution is the basic dogma of a non-theistic religion called Humanism that considers Christianity harmful to the common good and strides to replace it.

Thomas L. McFadden

Chapter 1- Americans Believe in Evolution

The one thing that most of the Catholic youth have in common with their fellow Americans is that they were taught, from the earliest days through high school, the materialistic evolutionary theory of origins as a scientific fact. They were taught that in public schools and in many (if not most) Catholic schools. That teaching is reinforced throughout our culture by science and nature- themed programs produced for the Public Broadcasting System (PBS), History Channel, Smithsonian Channel, and all public educational sites such as libraries, natural history museums and National Parks. The net result is that most students understand evolutionary origins to be a proved fact. Consider this college girl's understanding of origins: https://www.cal-catholic.com/west-valley-college-atheist-explains-her-concept-of-the-universe/

A Catholic reading this who also believes evolution to be a proved fact, may be wondering what this writer's problem is with that. Understandably so, because the majority of American Catholics accept that evolutionary theories of origins are factual. According to a study published in December 2013 by the Pew Research Center,

> Six-in-ten Americans (60%) say that "humans and other living things have evolved over time," while a third (33%) reject the idea of evolution, saying that "humans and other living things have existed in their present form since the beginning of time." The share of the general public that says that humans have evolved over time is about the same as it was in 2009, when Pew Research last asked the question.

The above result is summarized in Table 1 below. The report said that 68% of white, non-Hispanic Catholics believe that humans evolved from animals over time and just 26% believe that humans existed in present form since the beginning. The only groups with a higher belief in human evolution than white, non-Hispanic Catholics are the unaffiliated (76%) and mainline Protestants (78%). Among white Evangelical Christians, 64% believe that humans were created as they are now, just as the Fathers, Doctors, Councils and Popes have taught.

A follow up survey by Pew in 2014 found that belief in evolution continued to trend upward when compared to the results published in 2013 that were the basis for the discussion above.

TABLE 1

First Question	Second Question	April 2013	August 2014
Humans have Evolved		60%	65%
	Due entirely to natural process?	32%	35%
	Supreme Being guided evolution?	24%	24%
	Evolved but don't know how?	4%	5%
Humans have existed in present form since beginning		33%	31%
Don't Know		7%	4%

In the data from 2013 and 2014 above, an initial question asked respondents whether they think humans and other living things have evolved over time – in line with Charles Darwin's theory of evolution – or whether they believe humans have existed in their present form since the beginning of time, as in the Book of Genesis. Those who said they accept the idea of evolution then were asked a second question: whether they think evolution occurred due to natural processes such as natural selection, or due to processes that were guided or allowed by God.

In 2019 Pew Research experimented to see if the way the question was asked influenced the outcome. Half of the respondents were asked in a two-step process as described above. In the 2019 two-step process, the percentage of Catholics who believe in the special creation of human was about the same as in the 2014 survey, 29%. The other half were asked just one question but were asked to choose one of three possible replies that were offered to them. The single question was: "Which statement comes closest to your view?" The choices offered and the percentages of those choosing the answer are shown in the table below:

TABLE 2

Humans have evolved over time due to processes such as natural selection; God or a higher power had no role in this process	Humans have evolved over time due to processes that were guided or allowed by God or a higher power.	Humans have existed in their present form since the beginning of time
33% overall	48% overall	18% overall but Catholics 13%

Based on that data, 82% of American adults believe in evolution of humans from some sort of evolving animal. Pew, as an organization, has a bias in favor of evolution vs. *Genesis* which is obvious from the text describing evolution: "Humans have evolved over time due to processes such as natural selection." Natural selection as the mechanism for evolution is a scientifically dead proposition that continues in school textbooks and the imagination of social researchers who don't know any better. Natural selection is responsible for what is sometimes called "microevolution" or variations within a species such as. breeding of dogs wherein the variation results from remixing combinations present in the existing gene pool of dogs. Evolution theory proposes that mutations in the genes, if they result in enabling the organism a better chance to compete and survive, can add up, over millions and millions of years, and produce an entirely new species. That is called "macroevolution." That is a "scientific zombie" as will be explained later in this book.

Pew's report of the 2019 result emphasizes the drop in the percentage of those who answer that "Humans have existed in their present form since the beginning of time." depending on how the question is asked. As shown in Table 1 it was 33% in 2013 and 31% in 2014 for the two-step method. As shown in Table 2, with a single question and three choices to answer, it was 18% by all respondents and 13% by Catholic respondents.

Theistic Evolution

As noted in Table 2 above, perhaps 48 out of 100 American adults find a "third way" between the scientific consensus and the text of the Bible. While accepting that "something" turned into "everything" over billions of years, as taught to them in school, they overlay it with the belief that some Supreme Being guided evolution. The combination of belief in evolution as a proved scientific fact but then overlaid with belief in guidance by God at one or more points in, or prior to, a supposed multi-billion-year process defines the theistic evolution theory of origins. Among theistic evolutionists there is extreme vagueness about what those supernatural interventions were and when they happened. Some Catholics who hold that combination have been taught philosophical proofs for the existence of God and have been told that evolution was the playing out of secondary causes flowing according to Divine Providence from the original "whatever it

15

was" created from nothing "whenever." It "works" for them. Since they have reached mature adulthood and feel their Faith is fully intact, it is practically impossible to convince them that belief in evolution is causing others to lose their Faith. Many Catholics simply "tune out" to objections to evolution, such as the lack of scientific evidence, and other rational arguments such as "truth matters." Others accuse fiat creationists of being an embarrassment to the Church by being so "backward."

Axioms Instead of Evidence

The accusations of backwardness have been cast at Evangelical Protestants by the more "enlightened" within Protestantism for years. For example, in 2011 R. Albert Mohler Jr. was president of Southern Baptist Theological Seminary when he gave a public lecture in which he said the theory of evolution "represents one of the greatest challenges to Christian faith and faithfulness in our times." He disagreed with "the point made by so many others that we will actually lose credibility sharing the Gospel of Christ if we do not shed ourselves of the anti-intellectualism which is judged to be ours by the elite if we do not accept the theory of evolution." Typical of the "elite" is the Biologos Foundation which has enjoyed perceived scientific authority because it was founded and led by Francis Collins when he was Director of the National Institutes of Health. (Collins is the now-disgraced former Director who conspired with Dr. Anthony Fauci and others to cover up the fact that the NIH funded the development of the Wuhan virus that killed millions.)

BioLogos exists so that the evangelical church "can come to peace with the scientific data which shows unequivocally that the universe is very old and that all of life, including humankind, has been created through a gradual process that has been taking place over the past few billion years."

That statement by Biologos is an example of how evolutionists assert theories as unequivocal facts and treat them as axioms, a statement or proposition which is regarded as being established, accepted, or self-evidently true:

On the basis that what Biologos asserts about evolutionary cosmology and biology is self-evidently true, Karl Giberson, a senior fellow at BioLogos, wrote a response to Mohler's address:

> Is it not possible that you are simply caught in our current culture war, and have joined the 'anti-evolution' cause, mistakenly thinking you were defending the faith? In the big picture, though, I just cannot see why this is so important. You are asking Christians to reject modern science and alienate themselves from the educated world for a doctrine that seems so secondary."

Before the reader finishes chapters two and three of this book he will understand how terribly unscientific and speculative the gospel of Biologos is.

Dawkins: Theistic Evolutionists are Deluded

The same attitude prevails in parts of the Catholic intellectual and clerical community. This writer has been subjected to it by theology professors and parish priests. Belief in evolution often leads to a situation where Catholics lose respect for Catholics who dissent from Darwinian orthodoxy. Often this antagonism is associated with little understanding of the ideological bias of "evolutionary science," and how the "settled science" taught in school is so different from the science problems discussed in peer-reviewed professional journals. Relying on the maxim that "there can be no conflict between true science and true religion because God is author of both," many Catholic intellectuals, lay and clerical, sincerely believe that theistic evolution blends faith with scientific credibility. But the school kids are not "buying" it and the refusal to acknowledge that they aren't buying is self-

inflicted blindness. Richard Dawkins, world-famous evolutionary biologist, and atheist author (*The God Delusion, The Blind Watchmaker*) ridicules theistic evolutionists: "Theistic evolutionists are deluded." Watch this 1-minute video as Dawkins explains why
https://www.youtube.com/watch?v=BAbpfn9QgGA

Are Belief in Evolution and Apostacy Linked?

On December 14, 2021 Pew Research reported its latest survey in which it found that

> Currently, about three-in-ten U.S. adults (29%) are religious "nones" – people who describe themselves as atheists, agnostics or "nothing in particular" when asked about their religious identity. Self-identified Christians of all varieties … make up 63% of the adult population. Christians now outnumber religious "nones" by a ratio of a little more than two-to-one. In 2007, when the Center began asking its current question about religious identity, Christians outnumbered "nones" by almost five-to-one (78% vs. 16%)

The Perceived "Disconnect"

Our Sunday Visitor Weekly published on August 27, 2016, an article titled, "Young people are leaving the faith. Here's why: Many youths and young adults who have left the Church point to their belief that there is a disconnect between science and religion." The article was based on two national studies done by the Center for Applied Research in the Apostolate (CARA). The article said:

> The interviews with youth and young adults who had left the Catholic Faith revealed that the typical age for this decision to leave was made at 13. Nearly two-thirds of those surveyed, 63 percent said they stopped being Catholic between the ages of 10 and 17. Another 23 percent say they left the Faith before the age of 10. Those

18

who leave are just as likely to be male as they are female, and their demographics generally mirror those of all young Catholics their age. So why are they leaving?

According to the article they are leaving because of "science." The "disconnect between science and religion" means that the materialist explanation of origins resulting from cosmic and biological evolution taught in school destroys belief in the Bible and the supernaturalism upon which Catholicism depends. G. K. Chesterton wrote that "When men cease to believe in God, they do not then believe in nothing, they believe in anything."

When Pew interviewed people who had been raised Catholic and who now self-identified as unaffiliated it found that 48% of them lost their faith by age 18 and another 30% lost it by age 23. The specifically-Catholic studies by CARA cited earlier found the typical age at which Catholic children are lost is 13. At the very least that indicates the importance of counter-Catholic influences in formal schooling, which is the principal occupation of most persons younger than 18 and of many younger than 23.

Why They Say They Left

Pew Research published on August 24, 2016 a report called "Why America's 'nones' left religion behind" that said:

> About half of current religious "nones" who were raised in a religion (49%) indicate that a lack of belief led them to move away from religion. This includes many respondents who mention "science" as the reason they do not believe in religious teachings, including one who said "I'm a scientist now, and I don't believe in miracles." Others reference "common sense," "logic" or a "lack of evidence" – or simply say they do not believe in God.

Those responses identifying "science" are similar to those in the CARA studies.

Lack of Necessity May Lead to Unbelief

An article called "Scientists discover that atheists might not exist, and that's not a joke" on the website science20.com reviewed some studies from science journals. The opening lines were:

> Metaphysical thought processes are more deeply wired than hitherto suspected. While militant atheists like Richard Dawkins may be convinced God doesn't exist, God, if he is around, may be amused to find that atheists might not exist. Cognitive scientists are becoming increasingly aware that a metaphysical outlook may be so deeply ingrained in human thought processes that it cannot be expunged.

Those studies support anthropologists who have found that throughout all of history people of all civilizations have in some way believed in a Supreme Being. In other words, we are "wired" or "programmed" to believe in God. So why is doubt and indifference to God the fastest growing religion in America? In 1884 Pope Leo XIII identified the attack on faith caused by naturalism and evolutionism. And in a 1907 encyclical, "On the Doctrine of the Modernists" Pope St. Pius X described how evolution undergirded Modernism which he labeled "the synthesis of all heresies."

> First of all [the Modernists] lay down the general principle that in a living religion everything is subject to change, and must in fact be changed. In this way they pass to what is practically their principal doctrine, namely, evolution. To the laws of evolution everything is subject—dogma, Church, worship, the Books we revere as sacred, even faith itself, and the penalty of disobedience is death.

Phillip Campbell explained in his blog, *Unam Sanctam Catholicam*, that

> the reason Modernism is the synthesis of all heresies is not because it professes all heresies formally, but because of its incorporation of the principle of evolution as applied to truth. Darwin had presented the world with a model of reality which stressed becoming over being; in fact, there really was no "being" in the Aristotelian-Thomist sense. Every "being" was merely a moment in the history of becoming. That being the case, it was only so long before this concept was applied to revealed truth and even God Himself, and thus the Modernist theological school proposed that dogma can in fact evolve, not just in expression but in substance, which is a logical consequent of affirming the evolution of material substances. This is the sense in which Modernism is a synthesis of all heresies: because truth itself is subject to change, dogma becomes a potent medium for the impression of *any* teaching. Once the evolution of dogma is admitted, every heresy is present in potency.

Catholic philosophy professor Dennis Q. McInerny explained the connection between Modernism and evolution this way:

> Naturalism is a doctrine which simply denies the reality of the whole supernatural order; it goes hand in hand with materialism. One of the major outgrowths of naturalism was the theory of evolution, which was firmly set in place with the publication of Charles Darwin's *The Origin of Species* in 1859. More than just a scientific theory, evolutionism soon became for many a general philosophy of life, and the Modernists were much taken by it, welcoming it as a sterling manifestation of 'progressive' thought.

A Substitute Religion

Catholics who told the Pew researchers that "they just gradually drifted away" probably did not make a conscious decision and suddenly "stopped believing in Catholicism's teachings overall." The decision was made at a deeper level of consciousness. Never in those years of school did the textbooks and teachers need to explicitly say that God does not exist. It was sufficient to show He was unnecessary because the "big bang" and Darwinism explained to them their origin, existence, and physical reality better than the Catholicism they had learned. The worldview based on evolution is a substitute religion. And that religion with no God provides moral autonomy so "if it feels good, do it." Evolutionary biologist and best-selling atheist author Richard Dawkins explained that Darwinism makes theistic belief both implausible and unnecessary: "Darwin made it possible to be an intellectually fulfilled atheist." Dawkins claims to be one.

A school child will believe the story of evolutionary cosmic and biological origins because it is repeated by the authorities. Usually, no trusted adult will teach him differently. "The one who states his case first seems right, until the other comes and examines him" (*Proverbs* 18:17). Without adult help his belief in God can become skeptical. If God exists, then billions of years ago He put some physical laws in place, and has since practiced non-intervention in the natural behavior of the universe. The religious education he receives with its "miracle stories" is overshadowed with "science" that credits the formation of life and the universe to only natural processes. The homilies of priests, Church documents, CCD instruction materials, etc. invariably refer to or quote Bible texts with the assumption that those texts are taken at face value, i.e., "as gospel." That is no longer a safe assumption to which priests and others have not adjusted. To the teenagers wrestling with the scientific materialism drummed into them at school, instruction depending on "Bible stories" will seem facile. Put simply, church and CCD attendance does not a Christian make.

Many still-believing adult Catholics who were taught in school that cosmic and biological evolution ("big bang" and Darwinism) are scientific facts are reluctant to accept that such teaching could be a primary reason why others have lost their faith. Typically, they say it doesn't matter how everything got here as long as one believes "God did it." Nevertheless, the evidence that children are leaving in droves because instruction at school which credits evolution creates a perceived conflict with religion has been "stacked and catalogued." Yet, priests and parish Directors of Religious Education just keep doing the same things that have failed for the last 50 years. Catholic apologetics needs to embrace the 21st Century natural science that refutes those bogus 19th Century theories instead of "interpreting" the Bible to fit them. The creation doctrines that the spokesmen for the Church seem to have forgotten or misplaced must be taught again. The Humanist worldview and the confidence Humanists exude as they steamroll Christians in the public square is based on two affirmations of their faith, evolutionary cosmology, and evolutionary biology, that they have taught the majority of Catholics to accept, at least implicitly. In the following chapters evolutionary cosmology and biology will be considered.

Chapter 2-Evolutionary Cosmology

An illustration of theistic evolution--that combination of naturalism overlaid with supernaturalism--was published in a weekly Catholic newspaper revered by its subscribers for its fidelity to the Magisterium. The belief in that combination is proof that it "works" for some Catholics because it is unquestionably true that the man who wrote the illustrative article loves the Church. In his "First Teachers" column of January 22, 2015, in *The Wanderer*, James K. Fitzpatrick wrote:

> The Big Bang, which today we hold to be the origin of the world, does not contradict the intervention of the divine Creator, but, rather, requires it. Evolution in nature is not inconsistent with the notion of creation, because evolution requires the creation of beings that evolve.

The "Big Bang" is the centerpiece of evolutionary cosmology. What Mr. Fitzpatrick wrote is essentially what Pope Francis said around that time and Fitzpatrick was writing in support of Francis. Francis had no need for support. Although the "Big Bang" is not what the Catholic Church "holds" is the origin of the world it is taught in Catholic education as if is

What is the Origin of the "Big Bang" Theory?

Cosmology is a science that combines mathematics and theoretical physics to draw inferences from astronomical observations. Traditional cosmology from ancient times observed bodies moving throughout the observable range but thought of the size of the universe itself as static. Those unable or unwilling to accept that the universe was created and thus had a Creator asserted that the universe "just was." In other words, it was eternal without a beginning.

In the early 20th century, telescopic observations of distant starlight discovered a phenomenon known as the "red shift." Visible light is a particular series of different energy wavelengths and when light is broken into wavelengths the human eye sees them as different colors. (This can be seen by passing sunlight through a glass prism.) The longest of these wavelengths is seen as red. When astronomers scientifically observed starlight, it was noticeably "red" which indicated that they were seeing primarily the longest wavelengths. They reasoned that the wavelengths they saw were so long was because the source of the light was moving away from them at such speed that the wavelengths were "stretched." (The analogy of the "doppler effect" of sound waves is often given.) Thus, it was accepted that the universe was expanding at a very high rate of speed. If the universe was expanding, mathematicians such as Einstein made some assumptions about the history of the expansion and through mathematics calculated the growth (expansion) backward to a "beginning" from which the expansion began billions of years ago.

The Alternative to Divine Revelation

If one is intent on denying the Bible's supernatural explanation for the fiat creation of a complete universe just thousands of years ago and is willing to skip over the questions such as where did the matter and energy come from and what caused it all to expand and organize itself so well, it's a good working hypothesis. But it had so many technical problems it didn't really catch on until the 1960s when a "theory within the theory", that is, "inflation theory" abated some of the problems, at least within the math model. Of course, none of that was observed science and was just a mathematical construct loaded with assumptions including constants in the equations for which the values are unknown.

A Competitive Model of the Universe

In 1948 one of Britain's best-known astronomers, Sir Fred Hoyle, and two other Cambridge University physicists countered with the "steady state" theory, a belief that the universe had no beginning or end, but always existed and would continue to exist. Atheists/Humanists, as Hoyle was, rejected any theory that seemed to teach a beginning for the universe because that would point to a Beginner. That bias was so strong that they promoted a theory that violates the fundamental Law of Conservation of Mass/Energy, which states that mass/energy in the universe can neither be created nor destroyed. Hoyle's theory required a continual spontaneous stream of hydrogen atoms from nothing. Because the appearance of the rapid expansion of the universe exceeded the predictions of Hoyle's theory, and because of their reluctance to accept a theory dependent on violation of that conservation law, many astrophysicists began to postulate that an explosion of highly dense matter was the beginning of all space and time. In his 1950 BBC radio series, *The Nature of the Universe*, Hoyle mockingly called this idea the "big bang," considering it preposterous. Yet the theory—and the derisive term—have become mainstream, not only in astronomy but in culture as well. Because of the one and only correspondence between the Bible and the big bang, namely, that time had a beginning, the atheist big bang believers were called "evangelicals" by the atheist steady state believers.

What is the Purpose of that Theory?

The Big Bang is an attempt to explain the universe as a purely material event. The Big Bang Theory proposes that, at some moment, 13.7 billion years ago, all of space, energy and matter was contained in a dense and hot single point called "the singularity" from which the universe has been expanding and cooling ever since.

The "singularity theorems" are the work of Cambridge University physicists Roger Penrose and Stephen Hawking published in 1970. Joined by physicist George Ellis, the trio produced in 1973 equations that implied a singularity at the beginning of the universe where the density of matter and the curvature of space would approach an infinite. According to the theory, time and space began with the Big Bang. The "singularity" existed before time in no space.

There is no scientific consensus regarding the source and cause of that dense mass and the intense heat energy in that imagined single point. Popular and student-oriented literature treats "the big bang" as an axiom, that is, something so well established that students don't need an explanation for it. The problem of the origin of whatever caused the beginning or the source of the matter and energy is glossed over. All models include features contrary to known physical laws but compensates for them by theorizing the existence of things such as "dark matter" and "dark energy," neither of which has ever been observed. To fit the theory those two undetectable opposing "dark" forces have been theorized: Dark energy is pulling the universe apart; dark matter keeps the galaxies together. Stars in a galaxy of stars whirling about a center experience centrifugal force that ought to cause them to fly away from the center. But they don't. Current theories must add vast amounts of a hypothetical mass, called dark matter, to explain why galaxies are not torn apart by centrifugal forces. If this seems weird, Jake Hebert, physics Ph. D., provides perspective:

> Cosmology is the study of the origin and structure of the universe. Because the Big Bang is the dominant cosmological model, most astronomers interpret all their observations to fit this paradigm. Big Bang cosmology is filled with several strange concepts, including *inflation, dark energy, dark matter,* and a *multiverse*. While valid

27

scientific concepts such as quantum mechanics and relativity can indeed seem strange or counterintuitive, strange notions can also result from attempts to prop up a dying theory. Much of the weirdness of modern cosmology stems from an attempt to force the data to fit the Big Bang. Cosmology can be somewhat intimidating to non-specialists, but when one considers the reasons that Big Bang cosmologists invoke strange concepts like inflation, it quickly becomes apparent that the Big Bang is in trouble.

An article published November 8, 2017 by the top-tier science magazine, *Nature*, gave a glimpse of the kind of "trouble" with the Big Bang. "Dark-matter hunt fails to find the elusive particles: Physicists begin to embrace alternative explanations for the missing material."

> Physicists are growing ever more frustrated in their hunt for dark matter — the massive but hard-to-detect substance that is thought to comprise 85% of the material Universe. Teams working with the world's most sensitive dark-matter detectors report that they have failed to find the particles, and that the ongoing drought has challenged theorists' prevailing views.

That followed an article published in *Nature* on August 24, 2016, "Dark-matter evidence weakens" that reported: "A survey of X-ray light from galaxy clusters has found no evidence of dark matter decaying, in the latest in a series of contradictory results."

Nature, Oct. 2, 2020 in "Last chance for WIMPs: physicists launch all-out hunt for dark-matter candidate" reported that:

> For decades, physicists have hypothesized that weakly interacting massive particles (WIMPs) are the strongest

candidate for dark matter — the mysterious substance that makes up 85% of the Universe's mass. But several experiments have failed to find evidence for WIMPs, meaning that, if they exist, their properties are unlike those originally predicted.

The Missing Antimatter

According to the 'big bang' theory equal amounts of matter and antimatter should have formed. Antimatter is the same as matter except that each particle has the opposite charge, magnetic moment, etc. For instance, the antiparticle for the negatively charged electron is the positively charged positron. Antimatter is supposed to be an exact counterpart to matter, down to the same mass. This has been verified when it was shown experimentally that a proton and an antiproton have the same mass to within one part in 10 billion. Apparently minuscule particles of "antimatter" can be made in large scale laboratory experiments like those conducted using the Large Hadron Collider (LHC), the world's most powerful particle accelerator that is in Switzerland. The problem is that, so far, no antimatter domains have been detected in space within 6,523,127,520 light years distance from the Earth. In a 1998 article in *Science*, "Theorists nix distant antimatter galaxies," Samuel Ting, one of the leading advocates in the search for antimatter in space, lamented:

> At the beginning, equal amounts of matter and antimatter were created [in the "big bang"]. Now there seems to be only matter. There have been theoretical speculations about the disappearance of antimatter, but no experimental support.

Newsweek 10/25/17 summarized the finding published in *Nature* that "The Universe should not actually exist, CERN scientists discover."

After performing the most precise experiments on antiprotons that have ever been carried out, researchers have discovered a symmetry in nature that they say just shouldn't be possible.

According to an article in *Nature*, March 21, 2019, "Physicists see new difference between [the behavior of] matter and antimatter," several teams experimenting at the LHC are attempting to discover even a slight difference between the properties of matter and antimatter which could explain [to themselves and other materialists] why anything exists at all.

> As far as physicists know, matter and antimatter should have been created in equal amounts in the early Universe and so blasted each other into oblivion. But that didn't happen, and the origin of this fundamental [infinite] "imbalance" remains one of the biggest mysteries in physics. Antimatter has so far proved maddeningly identical to matter, and many physicists think it will remain that way, because any difference would shake the foundations of modern physics.

In conclusion, physical laws indicate that equal amounts of matter and antimatter would have been created in the proposed 'big bang.' As time goes by the research problems of the missing antimatter, and non-detection of dark matter, dark energy, and many more dark entities starts to indicate that the whole paradigm itself is in doubt, an implication that Catholics promoting the "big bang" are unwilling to entertain.

John Hartnett, Ph.D., a physics and cosmology professor at the University of Adelaide in Australia explained why cosmology got weird:

> This ludicrous situation has developed in astrophysics because of the initial assumption of *materialism* (matter

and energy is all there is) and the dogmatic insistence that it must be rigorously applied to the origin and structure of this universe. As a result, when physicists observe the rotation speeds of stars—not only in our own galaxy but also in many thousands of other spiral galaxies—they find that the stars in the spiral disks are moving too fast.

To fix this, the standard approach is to posit the existence, around every galaxy, of a spherical halo of dark matter that has just the right density, distribution, and gravitational properties to solve the conundrum but neither emits nor interacts with electromagnetic radiation. Because astrophysicists cannot explain these high rotational velocities with standard tried-and-tested Newtonian physics, they have concocted the notion that galaxies really comprise between 80% to 90% dark matter—stuff that is everywhere but we cannot see or detect it by any method.

Beginning about 200 years ago, scientists started to abandon the Word of God as authoritative in such matters as the creation of the universe and hence it follows today that they believe in materialism—that there is no Creator and the universe just created itself from nothing. The alternative to accepting the materialists' explanation is to consider the possibility that the universe is not as old as they imagine and that it was created only 6,000 years ago. For those fast stars this would mean they have not had time to fly apart.

Another "fast stars" problem that has been known to science since the 1950s is the "winding-up dilemma." For an easily-followed short video that describes the "winding-up dilemma," watch this: www.youtube.com/watch?v=KuUS6gWDYvE

If you want to ponder 14 more scientific reasons to doubt the claim that the universe is "billions and billions" of years old and that the Earth is over 4 billion years old, read this
https://www.icr.org/article/evidence-for-young-world/

Some Christians have been led to accepting a 14-billion-year-old cosmos because of the so-called "starlight problem." How could light from stars recently created be visible when they are millions of light years distant from Earth? ("Light years" is a measure of distance, not of time.) Albert Einstein determined that the speed of light is relative and essentially impossible to measure.

A similar question plagues the Big Bang: "How is it possible that areas of the universe 20 billion light years apart (in distance) are at the same temperature?" That is known as "the horizon problem." The horizon problem is explained here
https://creation.com/light-travel-time-a-problem-for-the-big-bang

Astronomers have proposed many solutions to it, but no satisfactory one has emerged to date. The original big bang theory assumed that the universe expanded at the same rate throughout history. But observation indicated that assumption left many problems such as the origin of large-scale structures like galaxies and the horizon problem. To "solve" those problems, in about the late 1970s, the inflation theory was tacked on to the big bang theory.

Inflation and the Borde-Guth-Vilenkin Theorem
Inflation says that the universe *has not* always expanded at the same rate, and that the universe has experienced many periods of brief but immense expansions faster than the speed of light in which the size of the universe nearly doubled. These periods, as said, were extremely short, lasting less than a second. After a single period, the expansion slowed down until the next rapid

inflation came and, again, massively increased the size of the universe. There is no coherent explanation for those sudden bursts of speed, or for that matter, what caused the big bang in the first place.

In the early 1990s a theory to incorporate "inflation" was embraced by two theoretical physicists at Tufts University and a decade later they were joined by Alan Guth, one of the original proponents of "inflation" which solved some problems in the singularity model. The BGV theorem reinforced the Hawking-Penrose-Ellis singularity theorem in proving that the universe had a temporal beginning. But as in all materialistic models it had no explanation for the origin of the matter and energy at the beginning. All materialistic models implicitly assert an effect without a cause or "causality without a cause."

18th Century Science Still Being Taught

In the excerpt below, from a report on Space.com, February 20, 2015, note how "clouds of gas" are said to explain the origin of the sun and stars.

> Earth's water has a mysterious past stretching back to the primordial clouds of gas that birthed the Sun and other stars. By using telescopes and computer simulations to study such star nurseries, researchers can better understand the cosmic chemistry that has influenced the distribution of water in star systems across the Universe.

"Primordial clouds of gas birthed the sun and other stars." That is the "nebular hypothesis" formulated by 18th Century German philosopher Immanuel Kant in his *Universal Natural History and Theory of the Heaven.* This proposes that the sun, the earth, and the rest of the solar system formed from a *nebula*, or cloud of dust and gas. The best- known pioneer of this was French deist mathematician Pierre-Simon Laplace (1749–1827) who restated and developed the nebular hypothesis. Three centuries later that is taught in schools as a fact simply because nothing better has come along and that hypothesis doesn't involve God. For example, on November 6, 2019 the prestigious science journal *Nature* printed an article "Primordial gas cloud has thoroughly modern make-up" which told its readers that

> Early in the history of the Universe, gas clouds birthed the first galaxies and stars. But the details of this process remain mysterious.

That is an example of a cosmic evolution axiom. In other words, it is understood to be so well-established that everyone "knows" it is true. However, despite the dogmatic support of a process that remains "mysterious" by evolutionary astronomers, it has a number of huge problems. For example, on December 10, 2015 *Nature* published research showcasing just some of those problems under the title "How the Solar System didn't form."

> Standard planet-formation models have been unable to reconstruct the distributions of the Solar System's small, rocky planets and asteroids in the same simulation. A new analysis suggests that it cannot be done.

https://www.nature.com/articles/nature16322#auth-1

In a review of that *Nature*-published research, John Hartnett, the aforementioned physics and cosmology professor at the University of Adelaide observed that

> That means no matter what the simulations are seeded with in terms of the size and mass distribution of the planetary embryos and planetesimals, the correct observed size, orbits and masses of the planets and the asteroid belt cannot be obtained from the same simulation. The simulations do not even start with the gas/dust nebular cloud from which the solar system is supposed to have evolved, but start at a point where it is assumed that planet-sized bodies have already formed

from accumulation of mass, thus skipping other potential problems. The 'embryos' present at the start of these simulations are 10 or 20 large planet-size bodies, and several thousand small planetesimals, at most a few hundred kilometers across.

Standard computer models have what is known as the "Mars problem." Hartnett's further explanation and discussion of "the Mars Problem" may be read here
https://creation.com/how-did-the-solar-system-form?f

The joint NASA-European space probe known as Cassini extensively explored Saturn and its rings for years. Analysis of the data showed it cannot be more than 100 million years old, not 4.5 billion years old. creation.com/saturns-system-still-young More info: https://creation.com/the-naturalistic-formation-of-planets-exceedingly-difficult. Also read
http://creation.com/stars-dont-form-naturally   And
http://www.icr.org/article/10347/

Most Observed Data Disagree with the Theories

For almost every solar system body the magnetic field strength is a surprise. Mercury should not have a magnetic field (but it does); surely Venus and Mars should have one like ours (but they don't); Jupiter's shouldn't be so strong; Saturn's shouldn't be so symmetrical; and Uranus' and Neptune's shouldn't be so *a* symmetrical. The geological behavior is frequently unexpected, too: volcanism on bodies too small to retain their heat for billions of years—Io, Pluto, Charon, and more. Io, a moon of Jupiter that is slightly larger than our moon, has 400 active volcanos. Then there is the exoplanet, 20% larger than Earth and twice the weight discovered in 2013 that should not exist, Kepler-78B. Read https://www.cfa.harvard.edu/news/2013-25

35

Essentially, the preferred naturalistic models for the development of our solar system cannot account for any of its major features. Scientists have been unable to explain even the closest body to the earth, the moon. The failure of naturalistic models is implicit support for the *Genesis* record of creation of the moon by God on the 4th day of creation, an idea unfortunately unthinkable to naturalists. For a debunking of the evolutionists' explanation of our solar system see "Our Created Solar System: What you are not being told." It is a great 1 and ½ hour presentation. https://www.youtube.com/watch?v=Gr8Az3QQZdI

The Foundation of Cosmology Overturned

Anyone who believes as I do that "The Word became flesh and dwelt among us" probably assumes that the Earth is a special place. Throughout most of history not only Christians thought so. And when they looked at the sun and stars apparently revolving around the Earth, it was logical to conclude that the Earth was the center of the universe. Scientific observations in the 16th century, particularly by Copernicus, called that notion into doubt. In the late 17th century, the scientific consensus accepted that the Earth actually revolved around the sun based on a publication in 1687 by Isaac Newton that combined mathematics with celestial observations. Newton conceptualized the Earth as a sphere in orbital motion around the Sun within an empty space that extended uniformly in all directions to immeasurably large distances. Eventually Einstein's 20th Century theory of relativity and scientific observations helped expand the scientific consensus to what is now the materialists' standard model for the universe's origin, namely, the Big Bang. Evolutionists cite three principal "clues" in support of the Big Bang: (1) The "redshift" of the light from distant galaxies that is interpreted as expansion of the universe, (2) how well the conditions stipulated by the BB, when combined with the standard model of particle physics, correctly predict the ratio of light elements in the universe, and

(3) the cosmic microwave background (CMB), which is microwave radiation that comes from all directions in space almost uniformly Almost invariably, whenever the CMB is mentioned either in technical journals or articles written for popular audiences it is stated as a matter of fact that the CMB is the "afterglow from the Big Bang" or similar phases. The understanding that the CMB comes from "all directions in space almost uniformly" led to the adoption by the scientific consensus of the Cosmological Principle which is

> the notion that the spatial distribution of matter in the universe is homogeneous and isotropic when viewed on a large enough scale, since the forces are expected to act uniformly throughout the universe, and should, therefore, produce no observable irregularities in the large-scale structuring over the course of evolution of the matter field that was initially laid down by the Big Bang.

Note that the Cosmological Principle consists of two assumptions: homogeneity and isotropy. In the cosmological sense, these assumptions mean that *the Earth does not enjoy a special vantage point in the universe.* To some, the Cosmological Principle has theological consequences. Stephen Hawking said

> "We are such insignificant creatures on a minor planet of a very average star in the outer suburb of one of a hundred billion galaxies. So it is difficult to believe in a God that would care about us or even notice our existence."

Earth, evolutionists say, as it evolved just happened, by purely random chance, to develop a unique and extraordinary combination of finely-tuned characteristics to support life. But what if one or both of those assumptions of which the Cosmological Principle consists is wrong and Earth is in a special place in the universe... such as its center?

One of those assumptions is that the universe is isotropic. *Isotropic* means that the cosmos looks pretty much the same no matter what direction you look in over sufficiently large distances. The proof suggested for that assumption is that the cosmic microwave which is everywhere in the universe and is detectable in the microwave part of the electromagnetic spectrum should be perfectly uniform all across the sky to, say, one part in 10,000. The background is measured by dividing the sky into parts and measuring cosmic microwave background in each part individually. These individual measurements are called dipoles (think of the north and south on a magnet) and they have direction (think of pointed arrows). It is expected that these dipoles have random orientations with no connection between them. That assumption was tested by measurements first done in a NASA project known as WMAP. Then the European Space Agency's Planck Mission with better instruments observed the cosmic microwave background (CMB) from 2009 to 2013. It improved upon and verified the WMAP data that all of the multipoles (arrows) point in all sorts of random directions *except the ¼ (known as the quadrupole) and the 1/8 (known as the octupole)* which are just a few degrees away from each other. The WMAP and Planck results were so contrary to expectations that among evolutionary cosmologists those two multipoles became known as the "Axis of Evil." Dr. Paul Sutter is an astrophysicist and chief scientist at the Ohio State University's Center for Science and Industry. He explained the significance of those findings in a 2017 post online https://www.space.com/37334-earth-ordinary-cosmological-axis-evil.html

As an evolutionist and Big Banger, he wasn't happy with them:

> This coincidence was first noted by NASA's early WMAP mission, but many dismissed it as a statistical fluke that would surely go away with better measurements. It didn't go away with better measurements. And it gets worse. It seems that the CMB is slightly cooler when viewed

through the "top half" of our solar system, and slightly warmer on the opposite side. I'm not talking much; just a handful of microKelvin difference, but it's measurable and definitely there. *Plus,* this peculiar relationship to our solar system is aligned with the quadrupole and octupole. That's odd. It's one thing for two of the multipoles to be aligned — maybe that's just random coincidence — but it's another for them to be associated with our solar system. Hence the nickname "Axis of Evil," a tongue-in-cheek reference to President George W. Bush's labeling of Iran, Iraq, and North Korea in 2002.

What's going on? The CMB shouldn't give two photons about our solar system — it was generated before the sun was a twinkle in the Milky Way's eye. [*This is how evolutionists talk.*] And we can't find any simple astrophysical explanation, like a random cloud of dust in our southern end that might interfere with the pristine cosmological signal in this odd way. Is it really just coincidence? Or does it seductively point the way to new and revolutionary physics? [Emphasis added.] Or maybe we just screwed something up with the measurements?

An article titled "Planck's most detailed map ever reveals an almost perfect Universe" that was published by the European Space Agency in March 21, 2013 began:

Acquired by ESA's Planck space telescope, the most detailed map ever created of the cosmic microwave background – the relic radiation from the Big Bang – was released today revealing the existence of features that challenge the foundations of our current understanding of the Universe...

But because precision of Planck's map is so high, it also made it possible to reveal some peculiar unexplained features that may well require new physics [Emphasis added] to be understood...One of the most surprising findings is that the fluctuations in the CMB temperatures at large angular scales do not match those predicted by the standard model – their signals are not as strong as expected from the smaller scale structure revealed by Planck.

Another is an asymmetry in the average temperatures on opposite hemispheres of the sky. This runs counter to the prediction made by the standard model that the Universe should be broadly similar in any direction we look.

Furthermore, a cold spot extends over a patch of sky that is much larger than expected.

The asymmetry and the cold spot had already been hinted at with Planck's predecessor, NASA's WMAP mission, but were largely ignored because of lingering doubts about their cosmic origin.

"The fact that Planck has made such a significant detection of these anomalies erases any doubts about their reality; it can no longer be said that they are artefacts of the measurements. They are real and we have to look for a credible explanation," says Paolo Natoli of the University of Ferrara, Italy.

The Planck data is so damaging to the standard model proposed for the universe by evolutionists that a member of the European Space Agency's team compared it to finding that the foundations of a house may be so weak as to topple the house:

"Imagine investigating the foundations of a house and finding that parts of them are weak. You might not know whether the weaknesses will eventually topple the house, but you'd probably start looking for ways to reinforce it pretty quickly all the same," adds François Bouchet of the Institut d'Astrophysique de Paris.

Also, in 2013 other scientists recognized the upheaval the Planck data caused in cosmological theory. For example, phys.org published "Discoveries from Planck may mean rethinking how the universe began." [Emphasis added.]

Recently, scientists on the Planck team announced finding certain large-scale features on the CMB sky that they cannot explain. One of them: a large cold spot, which corresponds to an anomalously large area of high density.

What does this mean? To discuss the findings, The Kavli Foundation held a discussion with three key members on the team. One important question: Will the theory for how the universe began need to be modified, amended or even fundamentally changed? [Emphasis added.]

"[T]he theory of inflation predicts that today's universe should appear uniform at the largest scales in all directions," says George Efstathiou, professor of Astrophysics at the University of Cambridge and director of the Kavli Institute for Cosmology at Cambridge (KICC). "That uniformity should also characterize the distribution of fluctuations at the largest scales within the CMB. But these anomalies, which Planck confirmed, such as the cold spot, suggest that this isn't the case."

Efstathiou has been involved in the Planck mission since it was first proposed to the European Space Agency in 1993. "[T]his is very strange," he says. "And I think that if there really is anything to this, you have to question how that fits in with inflation.... It's really puzzling."

Says Anthony Lasenby, a member of the Planck Core Team and professor of astrophysics and cosmology at Cambridge and Deputy Director of KICC: "[This] data is really putting pressure on some alternative inflation models.... Inflation actually may have been more limited in scope than previously theorized."

Says Krzysztof Gorski, a Planck Collaboration scientist and senior research scientist at the Jet Propulsion Laboratory in Pasadena, CA: "Perhaps we may still eliminate these anomalies with more precise analysis; on the other hand, they may open the door to something much more grand—a reinvestigation of how the whole structure of the universe should be." [Emphasis added.]

In an article published November 15, 2014 (https://arxiv.org/abs/1305.4134v1) theoretical physicist Ashok K. Singal of India's Space Research Organization's Physical Research Laboratory noted the totally unexpected and unexplainable clash between the data from the Planck mapping of the CMB and the assumption of isotropy (uniformity in all orientations):

We report the presence of large anisotropies [i.e., directionally dependent] in the sky distributions … in the 3CRR survey, the most reliable and most intensively studied complete sample of strong steep-spectrum radio sources. The anisotropies lie about a plane passing through the [Earth's] equinoxes and the north celestial pole. Two pertinent but disturbing questions that could be raised here are -- firstly why should there be such large anisotropies [directional dependencies] present in the sky distribution of some of the strongest and most distant discrete sources, implying inhomogeneities in the universe at very large scales (covering a fraction of the universe)? Secondly why should such anisotropies lie about a great circle decided purely by the orientation of earth's rotation axis and/or the axis of its revolution around the sun? Are these alignments a mere coincidence or do they imply that these axes have a preferential placement in the larger scheme of things, implying an apparent breakdown of the Copernican principle or its more generalization, cosmological principle, upon which the standard cosmological model is based upon?

In plain language, the Earth is probably the center of the universe. And the Cosmological Principle "upon which the standard cosmological model is based" is dead. For a more scientific discussion of the failed Cosmological Principle see German physicist Sabine Hossenfelder's explanation www.youtube.com/watch?v=JETGS64kTys

More trouble for the keystone assumptions behind the Big Bang explanation for the origin of the universe was reported on phys.org on November 5, 2019, "Researchers claim data from Planck space observatory suggests universe is a sphere."

> A trio of researchers with the University of Manchester, Università di Roma 'La Sapienza' and Sorbonne Universities has sparked a major debate among cosmologists by claiming that data from the Planck space observatory suggests the universe is a sphere—not flat, as current conventional theory suggests. In their paper published in the journal *Nature Astronomy*, Eleonora Di Valentino, Alessandro Melchiorri and Joseph Silk outline their arguments and suggest their findings indicate that there exists a cosmological crisis that must be addressed.
>
> Conventional theory, which backs inflation theory, suggests that after the Big Bang, the universe expanded in a way that was flat—two lights shone in parallel would travel forever in parallel. But now, after studying data sent back to Earth from the Planck space observatory (which mapped cosmic microwave background radiation over the years 2009 to 2013) Di Valentino, Melchiorri and Silk have come to disagree with conventional thinking. They claim that there is evidence that the universe is closed—that it is shaped like a sphere. If you shine two lights into the dark of space, they

suggest, at some point, the light would come back around to you from behind.

The researchers came to this conclusion after looking at data from the Planck space observatory that showed a discrepancy between the concentration of dark matter and dark energy and outward expansion; there was more gravitational lensing than theory has predicted. Such an imbalance, they claim, would have the universe collapsing in on itself, resulting in a sphere shape. Others who have looked at the same data prior to this new effort have called the data from the observatory a statistical fluke. The research trio note that there are other problems with the flat theory as well, such as scientists' inability to accurately measure the Hubble constant; each team that tries finds a different answer. There have also been problems with reconciling surveys of dark energy with a flat model. They conclude by acknowledging that with current technology there is no way to settle the debate— new devices will need to be invented that will be able to measure microwave background radiation in ways not subject to debate.

The Model is Broken in More Ways Than One

Since it was first put together in the 1970s, the standard model of physics has survived almost unchanged. An article in *Nature*, April 7, 2021 asked "Is the standard model broken" Physicists cheer major muon result." The article described the result of an experiment that "could ultimately force major changes in theoretical physics and reveal the existence of completely new fundamental particles."

Popular Science Story Spinning

Working scientists admit that the Planck Mission observations cast serious doubt upon the adequacy of the standard model of the universe by evolution from a "big bang," The popular media love to spin stories for the general public. As an example of how theoretical cosmology is stoked for the general public by story tellers consider "Ripples from the Big Bang," *NY Times*, March 24, 2014:

> When scientists jubilantly announced last week that a telescope at the South Pole had detected ripples in space from the very beginning of time, the reverberations went far beyond the potential validation of astronomers' most cherished model of the Big Bang.
>
> The ripples detected by the telescope Biceps2 were faint spiral patterns from the polarization of microwave radiation left over from the Big Bang. They are relics from when energies were a trillion times greater than the Large Hadron Collider can produce. These [radiation] waves are the long-sought markers for a theory called inflation, the force that put the bang in the Big Bang: an antigravitational swelling that began a trillionth of a trillionth of a trillionth of a second after the cosmic clock started ticking. Scientists have long incorporated inflation into their standard model of the cosmos, but as with the existence of the Higgs, proving it had long been just a pipe dream.

Within 6 months, this long-sought after sign of the presence of something supportive for the inflation theory (essential to the Big Bang theory) turned out to have been, literally, dust. An article entitled "Inflation, Elation, Deflation: Reflecting on BICEP2" on PBS, October 21, 2014, recounted how

> Six months ago astrophysicists working on an experiment called BICEP2 were celebrating what some called the discovery of the century: the detection of a specific polarization signature in the cosmic microwave background radiation that, interpreted conservatively, provided the most direct confirmation ever of cosmic

45

inflation. Read more expansively, it was seen as evidence for the quantization of gravity and the existence of the multiverse.

Last month, new data released by the Planck team confirmed that all or most of the BICEP2 signal could indeed be due to dust. It doesn't rule out the possibility that BICEP2 saw something real, but shows that the signal can't yet be untangled from the noise.

All of which has scientists and science media wringing their hands over what—if anything—they should have done differently. The splashy announcement, accompanied by literal and figurative champagne-cork-popping, as we covered here, coincided not with publication in a peer-reviewed journal but with the publication of results online. Should the authors have waited for peer review to announce their results? Should journalists have been more circumspect?

Indeed, and should Catholics also be more circumspect before reinterpreting *Genesis* to fit the claims of the secular Humanists?

Scientists Argue Over Big Bang

Watch this video in which 2 of the world's most famous theoretical cosmologists, Sir Roger Penrose and Sean Carroll, debate the question "Whether the universe began, as all our children are taught at school, with a big bang." The video explains how famous those two are.

https://www.youtube.com/watch?v=7HES3bPNAsA

Penrose effectively asserts that the universe created itself. He avoids questions about whether the universe had a beginning by walking it back through a series of expansions and collapses which presumably go back infinitely. Carroll, from the California Institute of Technology, begins his presentation by assuring the audience that "the big bang model is true, there is no point in doubting the big bang model." But then over the next 37 minutes one learns about the assumptions and fudge factors in the model. Before they finish, they are speculating about multiple universes that may exist!

Watch it and learn that it is all speculation and how hard these experts try to avoid talking about the origin of it all, namely, the First Cause Who revealed to us His supernatural creation by His will. *Creation ex Nihilo.* ("creation from nothing") refers to the moment God created something (the universe) from nothing (that which lacks matter, energy, space, and time).

The Bible implies *creation ex nihilo* in Genesis but Hebrews 11:3 states it explicitly, "The universe was framed by God's command, so that what is seen was not made out of what was visible." "Seen" and "visible" refer to the stuff investigators can and do detect, namely space, time, matter, and energy. Promoters of the big bang theory who are evolutionists are killing the faith of Catholic children in the Bible.

Big Bang Bunk Spreaders

It is amazing how many Catholic intellectuals have not merely tolerated the 'big bang' idea, but embraced it. They brag that it was first proposed in 1927 by the Belgian Catholic priest Georges Lemaître.   To hear their pronouncements, believers should welcome it as a major plank in our defense of the faith. "At last, we can use science to prove there's a creator of the universe." Belief in the existence of a God on the evidence of reason and nature alone, with rejection of supernatural revelation, is deism. A good example close to that school of thinking is Big Bang Jesuit Robert Spitzer with his video "Nothing to Cosmos: God and Science." Another "big banger" who also teaches that the Bible is not inerrant is lay theologian Christopher Baglow. Baglow has spread "scientific" ignorance and religious error via

47

video lectures featured in a "Catholic" program called "That Man is You" sold by Paradisus Dei, LLC to Catholic Men's groups. His lectures are full of statements that one who knew anything much about evolutionary theories or Catholicism would refute easily, but how does one interrogate a video presentation?

The Big Bang hypothesis requires that most of the matter in the universe must be something that has never been observed by natural science. The Big Bang's assumption-based hypotheses are constantly subject to change to explain the pre-historic past by observations of the present. These cosmic hypotheses are not scientific theories because they do not meet the criteria required to be a scientific theory. Scientific theories are testable and make falsifiable predictions. It is a fool's errand to try to test "cosmic evolution." One cannot overturn a metaphysical commitment like the "big bang" by evidence because that commitment wasn't arrived at via evidence. Sir Fred Hoyle readily saw through the fallacious assumptions. In 1994 he wrote, "Big-Bang cosmology refers to an epoch that cannot be reached by any form of astronomy, and, in more than two decades, it has not produced a single successful prediction." Explanations of the Big Bang must be taken on faith (called "science") while other faith-based explanations, such as given in Divine Revelation, are blown off by "sophisticated" Catholics."

The Search for Possible Life Is Based on Evolution Theory

Big Bang cosmology thrives at taxpayer expense among Humanist scientists in academia and the Federal Government. Consider NASA's $692M evolutionary hope scheme "Exoplanet Exploration" as an example of a misplaced fiscal priority. It was driven by Humanist religious zeal to find life somewhere in the universe to validate (in their minds) that Earth is not unique and not the place where its Creator dwelt for 33 years. According to William Borucki, principal investigator for NASA's Kepler mission speaking in 2009: "If we find lots of planets like ours…we'll know it's likely we aren't alone, and someday we might be able to join other intelligent life in the universe." The Kepler spacecraft took wonderful pictures and found more than 2,680 exoplanets orbiting distant stars before it died in 2018 after 9 years. An article in the *New Scientist,* March 22, 2019, "We've found 4000 exoplanets but almost zero are right for life" summarized the situation: follows:

> We have found more than 4000 planets orbiting distant stars, but it turns out that probably none of them have the right conditions for life to evolve, making Earth even more special than we thought.

The launch of the James Webb Space Telescope (JWST) on Christmas 2021 brought new hope to those seeking life somewhere in space. For example, on December 14, 2022 *Nature* published "JWST gets first glimpse of 7-planet system with potentially habitable worlds, Astronomers have been eager for the landmark telescope to study the TRAPPIST-1 system." But by June 19, 2023 *Nature* reported the disappointment: "Life in the cosmos: JWST hints at lower number of habitable planets. Observations from the James Webb Space Telescope suggest that a second world in a seven-planet system lacks an atmosphere."

> For the second time, the James Webb Space Telescope (JWST) has looked for and failed to find a thick atmosphere on an exoplanet in one of the most exciting planetary systems known. Astronomers report[1] today that there is probably no tantalizing atmosphere on the planet TRAPPIST-1 c, just as they reported months ago for its neighbor TRAPPIST-1-b.
> There is still a chance that some of the five other planets in the TRAPPIST-1 system might have thick atmospheres containing geologically and biologically interesting compounds such as carbon dioxide, methane, or oxygen. But the two planets studied so far seem to be without, or almost without, an atmosphere. Because planets of this type are common around many stars, "that would

definitely reduce the number of planets which might be habitable," says Sebastian Zieba, an exoplanet researcher at the Max Planck Institute for Astronomy in Heidelberg, Germany.

School Children are Told a "Well-Known Story"

An article in *Scientific American*, April 30, 2019, "Cosmology Has Some Big Problems" observed that the cosmology field "relies on a conceptual framework that has trouble accounting for new observations."

> This well-known story [the Big Bang] is usually taken as a self-evident scientific fact, despite the relative lack of empirical evidence—and despite a steady crop of discrepancies arising with observations of the distant universe... A crucial function of theories such as dark matter, dark energy, and inflation—each in its own way tied to the big bang paradigm—is not to describe known empirical phenomena but rather to maintain the mathematical coherence of the framework itself while accounting for discrepant observations. Fundamentally, they are names for something that must exist insofar as the framework is assumed to be universally valid.

The Big Bang is only a conundrum-riddled enigma that is the working hypothesis of theoretical physics that seeks a naturalistic explanation for the universe's existence.

Why do some Catholics, including priests and lay theologians teaching at nominally "orthodox" Catholic colleges, prefer that enigma to divine revelation? Mihael Chaberek, O.P., in his book *Aquinas and Evolution* asserts that they really don't understand the science and have a terrible fear of being considered anti-science so they go with the materialist explanations of origins but to show their orthodoxy they tell their students "God did it." The students don't "buy it" and many walk away.

Chapter 3-Evolutionary Biology

Moving on from the evolution-based cosmology to what the *Catechism* calls the many scientific studies which have splendidly enriched our knowledge of … the development of life forms *[abiogenesis theory]* and the appearance of man *[biological evolution from a common ancestor, i.e., Darwinism]*, consider how *The Wanderer* writer Fitzpatrick explained what he learned from his Catholic religious order teachers as a youth.

> I don't know if my experience is typical, but this is the understanding of the Book of *Genesis* that I have been taught since I was in high school in the Bronx in the 1950s. The Marist Brothers who taught me at that time would tell their students that Catholics are free to believe that evolution took place, as long as they understood it to be a process begun by God, and one in which human beings were created when God infused a soul into the evolving creature that became man. This was the same understanding taught to me by Jesuit priests at Fordham in the 1960s.

It is not surprising that the above non-scientific, non-Biblical explanation would have been taught by Jesuits given the present state of the Jesuits. Some Jesuits "got aboard," so to speak, with evolution long before evolution's most famous early expositor, Charles Darwin, was born. For example, in the late 18th Century, English Jesuit John Needham was the leading voice arguing that life could spontaneously arise from non-life.

Life from Non-Life Speculation Never Dies
Life arising from non-life, abiogenesis, is part of the faith package that comes with evolution. Fr. Needham would have rejoiced to hear Darwin suggesting in 1871 that the original spark

of life may have begun in a "warm little pond, with all sorts of ammonia and phosphoric salts, light, heat, electricity, etc. present, so that a protein compound was chemically formed ready to undergo still more complex changes." (We now know that water forms a chemical barrier to the formation of chains of nucleotides such as RNA and DNA.) Darwin's speculation is the origin of the "primordial soup" explanation for the beginning of life found in so many school textbooks and nature programs on PBS. The Primordial Soup Hypothesis was resurrected in 1936 by Russian chemist A. I. Oparin. He proposed how it could have happened if conditions on the earth back then (whenever back then was) were different than they were at present. Among other things, the proposed soup had to be in an oxygen-free atmosphere. The beauty of that speculation from the evolutionist view point is that it can be told to children without any need to prove it. And it cannot be disproved.

In 1952, a graduate student, Stanley Miller, and his professor tested Oparin's idea by mixing water and three gases in an oxygen-free environment, ran electricity through the mix and produced two amino acids. These are not alive but are chemical compounds integral to protein. That was the famous Miller-Urey experiment. So constantly repeated is the propaganda regarding the importance of that lab experiment that this writer has a friend with two science degrees who told him that that experiment had proved life can come from non-life. In 2000, Miller was working for NASA and trying to find ways to rescue the original scheme. For more on Miller-Urey see http://creation.com/life-in-a-test-tube . Also https://creation.com/origin-of-life-research

The PBS Evolution Project
A classic example of the "Life from Non-Life" (abiogenesis) propaganda that must have impressed the authors of paragraph 283 of the *Catechism* is the PBS Evolution Project. The Project

includes a seven-part television series, a web site, a multimedia library, and an educational outreach program. The TV series is "Evolution" and it was produced and first broadcast circa 2000. The companion book to the PBS Series is *Evolution: The Triumph of An Idea*. It is interesting that it was called the "triumph of an idea" rather than a "triumph of science." It supports this writer's contention that evolution is more about faith than science.

The importance evolutionists attached to the PBS Evolution Project is manifested by who was chosen to write the TV program's companion book's six-page Introduction. It was Stephen Jay Gould, the most famous evolutionist in America. He was Professor of Zoology and Professor of Geology at Harvard and the curator for invertebrate paleontology in that university's Museum of Comparative Zoology. He was at Harvard from 1967 until his death in 2002. As of 2002 he had published 22 books. He was also America's greatest communicator of evolutionary ideas to the ordinary laymen which he accomplished through more than 300 essays in *Natural History* magazine between 1974 and 2001. He was the consummate story spinner for he wrote interesting and captivating prose. In his Introduction to *Evolution: The Triumph of An Idea,* Gould started with an apocryphal story making fun of the wife of a Church of England clergyman. According to this story which took place in the "early days of Darwinism" the woman

> exclaimed to her husband when she grasped the scary novelty of evolution: 'Oh my dear, let us hope that what Mr. Darwin said is not true. But if it is true, let us hope that it will not become generally known!'

Then, despite the universities, public schools, media, and Federal Government dedicated to evolution propaganda Gould whined that evolution had not become generally known in the United States:

> For what Mr. Darwin said is clearly true, and it has also not become generally known (or, at least in the United States, albeit uniquely in the Western world, even generally acknowledged). We need to understand the reasons for this exceedingly curious situation.

As noted earlier in this book, Pew Research indicates that as of 2019, perhaps 82% of adult Americans believe evolution is a fact. To see why not everyone is fooled, read "Can Darwinian Evolutionary Theory Be Taken Seriously?" http://natureinstitute.org/txt/st/org/comm/ar/2016/teleology_30.htm

Evolution: The Triumph of An Idea begins with a narrative of Darwin's history, the compatibility of his thought with that of his many contemporaries, and the ridicule by PBS of those who disagreed with him. And those who disagreed were more numerous. For example, Scotsman James Clerk Maxwell (1831-1879) was one of the greatest scientists who have ever lived. In presenting a paper, "Discourse on Molecules." to the British Association at Bradford in 1873 he pointed out that

> No theory of evolution can be formed to account for the similarity of molecules, for evolution necessarily implies continuous change .... The exact equality of each molecule to all others of the same kind gives it ... the essential character of a manufactured article, and precludes the idea of its being eternal and self-existent.

PBS is correct that Darwin's ideas became the centerpiece of a naturalistic scientific consensus that has culturally, if not scientifically, triumphed. The PBS evolution extravaganza provides an opportunity to illustrate life from non-life propaganda by reference to where it was transferred into print in the companion book. That is in the book's section, "In Search of Life's Origins" (pages 104-115).

Life from Space Debris

On the first page is an artist's conception drawing of a bright object moving against a background of what looks like a night sky full of stars. The caption on the picture is "Comets may have seeded the early Earth with many of the building blocks of life." That speculation would be called a scientific theory by evolutionists. When interviewed by Ben Stein in the movie *Expelled,* Richard Dawkins said that space aliens from a technically advanced civilization may have put the building blocks on the comet. The term "building blocks" is a scientific trivialization typical of evolutionary story telling. There are no "building blocks" to be stacked up or mixed up to produce life. Life is on a completely different order from the components that make it up. A child watching this on TV might accept seed-bearing comets as science. Should we?

Life from the Hot Tub

On the next page there is a truly beautiful picture of a hot spring at Yellowstone Park surrounded by snow just at dawn. The caption is "Hot springs in Yellowstone are home to some of the most primitive microbes on Earth. Researchers suspect that life may have begun 4 billion years ago in near-boiling water." That's Darwin's "warm little pond" speculation from 1871 updated with 21st Century audio-visual effects. Who would those unnamed researchers be and what observed data supports their suspicion? Again, one can see evolutionary story telling in the term "primitive microbes." If they are very simple and basic, how did they become alive and then get all of the genetic material to become our ancestors? All evolutionary writing is aimed at communicating more than is actually written. In this caption, it doesn't actually say that the microbes in the spring are evidence of anything at all. But with the beautiful picture and the professional narrator, what child would not infer what the script writer wanted to be inferred?

The Space Debris Assembles Itself

The text on the pages is equally pseudo-science. For example,

> The first step in the rise of life was to gather its raw materials together. Many of them could have come from space. Astronomers have discovered a number of basic ingredients for life on meteorites, comets, and interplanetary dust.

The above asserts that life arose in a series of steps. Unstated is who or what is the active agent taking the "first step" of gathering raw materials together because there was no life. The evolution story, like all false ideologies, begins with a bald assertion which is then treated as a fact upon which the story is built. From here on there will be a lot of "could have" and "may have" speculation statements that build on the initial bald assertion.

> As these objects fell to the early Earth, they could have seeded the planet with components for crucial parts of the cell, such as the phosphate backbone of DNA, its information-bearing bases, and amino acids for making proteins.

One wonders how the information got into the "information-bearing bases." Only intelligence can produce such information.

> As these compounds reacted with one another, they may have produced more life-like forms.

That sentence puts it out there for belief of the gullible that non-living things falling to earth could have produced life-like forms. The term "life-like forms" is jargon that means nothing. But the scary thing is that the theologians and bishops who collaborated on the *Catechism* would teach the faithful that there are "many scientific studies which have splendidly enriched our knowledge of … the development of life forms." The PBS story continued:

> Chemical reactions work best when the molecules involved are crowded together so they bump into one another more often; on the early Earth, the precursors of biological matter might have concentrated in raindrops or the spray of ocean waves.

The assertion above is leading to an assertion to be made later in this fantasy story that non-biological material evolved into biological material by chemical reactions.

> Some scientists suspect that life began at the midocean ridges where hot magna emerges from the mantle. The branches nearest to the base of the tree of life, they point out, belong to bacteria and archaea that live in extreme conditions such as boiling water or acids. They may be relics of the earliest ecosystems on the planet.

"Some scientists suspect" is one of the most hackneyed phrases of the evolution genre. It conveys the aura of scientific knowledge and authority but doesn't actually have anything behind it. The paragraph above doesn't actually say how the bacteria and archaea came to life but a child could infer more than has actually been said. A college student might ask: "Do you suspect, professor, that if something is not living and you boil it in hot magna it will become a living thing?" If he says "yes" the student ought to ask for a tuition refund.

> Scientists suspect that prebiological molecules became organized into cycles of chemical reactions that could sustain themselves independently. A group of molecules would fashion more copies of itself by grabbing other molecules around it.

How can molecules organize? One of the fundamental laws of science, the Second Law of Thermodynamics, is that material tends toward disorganization. How could lifeless molecules know how to grab molecules around them, or which ones to grab, to make copies of themselves? How would they "know" when the grabbed molecules constitute a copy of themselves?

The next paragraph is asserting chemical to biological evolution.

> There may have been many separate chemical cycles at work on the early Earth. If they used the same building blocks to complete their cycles, they would have competed with each other. The most efficient cycle would have outstripped the less efficient ones. Before biological evolution, in other words, there was chemical evolution.

That last sentence doesn't actually say that biological life resulted from chemical evolution but that is what was implied because that is part of the evolutionist story telling for the public. Almost no mainstream evolutionary biologist proposes chemical evolution as the source of first life. In the next chapter of this book, you will read that an evolution-believing chemist of note labels that as "astonishingly improbable."

> Ultimately, these molecules gave rise to DNA, RNA, and proteins.

Ultimately, the tooth fairy came, took my tooth, and left DNA under my pillow. It's as simple as that. "Ultimately" according to evolutionists, the most complex things just "rise."

Amazing Information-Rich DNA

DNA is so amazingly complex that this writer will only touch on its importance. As much as anyone would ever want to know can be found in *Darwin's Doubt* by Stephen Meyer. Meyer reveals from the research of modern science a cellular complexity that was undreamed of 50 years ago when the evolution myth with its simplistic story became educational orthodoxy in America. The PBS tooth fairy science story said "information-bearing bases" could have been included in the "basic ingredients for life on meteorites, comets, and interplanetary dust." Those "information-bearing bases" of DNA are the genetic code. Information is created only by an intelligent mind. Complexity alone does not necessitate intelligence, but something called *specified complexity* does. In other words, there is of necessity a very specific pattern or complexity that must occur in the configuration. Genetic code provides a classic example of this. Individual genes must be arranged in very specified patterns. Every gene needs to be located in a specific place for genes to function properly. The configuration is not just complex but also specified. If the re-discovery and validation at the beginning of the 20th Century of genetic laws demonstrated by Mendel in the 1860s gave Darwinism a kick in the teeth, the discovery of DNA in 1953 would have buried it if any of this had anything to do with science. Darwinism, in one or more of its latest syntheses, can no more be removed from Humanist religion than the Incarnation can be removed from Christianity.

In the decades that followed, much genetic research has been completed. The most important of that is sponsored and funded by the National Institutes of Health's National Human Genome Institute

In 2005 science even discovered that there is an epigenetic code behind the DNA code! The more science learns about epigenetic and DNA information the more troublesome it becomes for evolutionists to tell their fables. A great article called "The Genetic Puppeteer" about how the epigenetic code controls the DNA code is at http://creation.com/the-genetic-puppeteer.

Nearly two decades after the initial sequencing of the human genome, a multi-million-dollar, multi-institutional program finished its final reporting. This was the Genotype Expression Project (GTEx). The goal of this 10-year study was to look at variations in the genome and see how they affect RNA production, phenotype, and disease. Read about it https://creation.com/human-genome-amazingly-complex

Primordial Soup Still on the Menu

Prestigious universities are still ladling out the primordial soup story to gullible students along with the "Tree of Life" fantasy. For example, the U. of California at Berkley had online in 2016 "Understanding Evolution: your one-stop source for information about evolution." Evolution 101 features a learning module called "From Soup to Cells- The Origin of Life." It is like the tooth-fairy science spun by PBS in 2000.

Pre-DNA Assumptions

As far back as the 1930s evolutionists put a number on the so-called "human mutation rate." The rate is key to calibrating the evolutionists' "molecular clock" that puts dates on events in evolutionary history. That became the basis for stories about how tens of thousands of years ago "in humanity's past, a small group of homo sapiens migrated out of Africa before spreading out to every possible corner of the Earth."

Stories like that became "facts" decades before DNA was identified as one of the carriers of encoded genetic information. This was the state of science that informed the teachers of schoolboys Mr. Fitzpatrick, Pope John Paul II, Benedict XVI, Francis, and the teachers of generations after them, as they parroted evolutionary time-scales as facts.

An article in *Nature* on March 10, 2015 reported that the new research in the last six years showed a "human mutation rate" about half of the rate that had been the scientific consensus. This really messes up the evolutionary "tree of life," descent from common ancestor fiction. An article, also in *Nature* and published in September 2012, explained why:

> Although a slowed molecular clock may harmonize the story of human evolution, it does strange things when applied further back in time," says David Reich, an evolutionary geneticist at Harvard Medical School in Boston, Massachusetts. "You can't have it both ways. For instance, the slowest proposed mutation rate puts the common ancestor of humans and orangutans at 40 million years ago," he says: more than 20 million years before dates derived from abundant fossil evidence. This very slow clock has the common ancestor of monkeys and humans co-existing with the last dinosaurs. "It gets very complicated," deadpans Reich.

Bad and Uncertain

One of the organizers of the conference described in the March 2015 article in *Nature*, David Reich, the population geneticist from Harvard, presented the results of two recent studies which had calculated a "slow rate" and another which had calculated an "intermediate rate." He said he was unable to explain the difference and at that point he injected the only moment of reality into the conference when he was quoted as having said

> The fact that the clock is so uncertain is very problematic for us...It means that the dates we get out of genetics are really quite embarrassingly bad and uncertain.

Evolutionists "know" that humans have been around for hundreds of thousands of years. Therefore "much of the meeting revolved around when the mutation rate accelerated and decelerated — and why." Have they ever considered that maybe humans have not descended from anything and have only been here for 6000 years or so?"

Mutations Are Winding Us Down

The most puzzling part of the genetic "human mutations rate" discussion is the mixture of the theory that humans descended from some non-human ancestor (meaning that they added genetic information to become a different species through mutations), with the real observations that humans only develop mutations with harmful effects and pass them on to following generations (meaning that humans are becoming more genetically flawed). Calling someone a mutant is an insult because mutations, which are copying mistakes in DNA, are almost always bad. In fact, many mutations are known by the diseases they cause. In *Genetic Entropy and the Mystery of the Genome* former Cornell University professor Dr John Sanford pointed out the seriousness of this problem. He showed that mutations are rapidly decaying the information within the human genome. According to evolutionary theory, mutations coupled with natural selection, is the means by which new information arises. But, according to Sanford, if mutation and selection cannot preserve the information already in the genome it's difficult to imagine how it created all that information in the first place. See https://creation.com/genetic-entropy-vs-evolution

The May 2015 issue of *Discover*'s cover story was "Evolution Gone Wrong: Why Humans Struggle to Adapt to Modern Diseases." The article is full of evolutionary bravado, including assuring readers that "humans are still evolving," but featuring the concerns of Harvard evolutionary biologist Daniel Lieberman who has coined the new term, dysevolution, to describe the degenerating state of human health as disease is passed through inheritance.

For those interested in a very technical discussion of why mutations can't explain the supposed evolution of humans from some other "ancestor," read
http://www.creationwiki.org/Haldane%27s_Dilemma

A Constantly-Shifting Contradictory Fairy Tale

Scientific American's September 2014 Special Evolution Issue provided an article "The Human Saga: Evolution Rewritten" that said "awash in fresh insights, scientists have had to revise virtually every chapter of human history." The scientists to whom the article refers are not empirical scientists; they are "pre-historic" scientists who dig up fossils and make interpretations according to *a priori* strictures. Those strictures require that human descent from animals is a fact. The article features the usual artist drawing of the supposed "Human Family Tree" of skull fragments, all distinct with no transitional forms, and this commentary on that imagined "tree."

> With relatively few fossils to work from, scientists' best guess was that they all could be assigned to just two lineages, one of which went extinct and the other of which ultimately gave rise to us. Discoveries made over the past few decades have revealed a far more luxuriant tree, however-one abounding with branches and twigs that eventually petered out. This newfound diversity paints a much more interesting picture of our origins but makes sorting out our ancestors from the evolutionary dead ends all the more challenging, as paleoanthropologist Bernard Wood explains in the pages that follow.

On the following pages the story notes that because of the fossils found in the last 40 years "figuring out how they are all related— and which one led directly to us—will keep paleontologists busy for decades to come." In other words, they do not a clue but as long as they have a theory, it is "science."

Warning for Would-Be Polygamists: It Is Hard Work

The stuff that appears in tooth-fairy science magazines can be fun. For example, the above-mentioned Special Evolution Issue of *Scientific American* also featured an article called "Powers of Two." The article describes a study by scientists who say they discovered how monogamy evolved in human culture. According to anthropologist C. Owen Lovejoy of Kent State University

> Soon after the split from the last common ancestor between the great ape and human evolutionary branches more than seven million years ago, our predecessors adopted a transformative trio of behaviors: carrying food in arms freed by bi-pedal posture, forming pair bonds, and concealing external signals of female ovulation. Evolving together, these innovations gave hominins, the tribe that emerged when early humans diverged from chimpanzees a reproductive edge over apes...an ancestral polygamous mating system was replaced by pair bonding when lower-ranked hominin males diverted energy from fighting toward finding food to bring females as an incentive to mate. Females preferred reliable providers to aggressive competitors and bonded with the better foragers. Eventually the females lost the skin swelling or other signs of sexual receptivity that would have attracted different males while their partners were off gathering food.

This "science" covers two pages in the text but was summed up by three sentences in very large type:

> Keeping many mates is hard work. It involves a lot of fighting with other males and guarding females. Monogamy might have emerged as a way to reduce the effort.

Perhaps the Kent State anthropologist discovered how evolution happened by "survival of the laziest."

Chapter 4-Why That Was Important

One purpose of this book is to encourage Catholics to have confidence in God's Revelation in the Bible. Contrary to the opinion of those who wrote paragraph 283 of *The Catechism*, science has not "splendidly enriched our knowledge of the development of life forms and the appearance of man." The Humanists abuse us and run the country based on having convinced many of us that science and history are on their side. But the PBS fantasy "In Search of Life's Origins," and other evolutionary tales you just read is the best explanation Humanists have for the origin of life and human history. That which modern science is learning challenges that nonsense.

In the last chapter I showed how the PBS Evolution Project suggested that life evolved from chemicals. To appreciate how evolution propaganda is so far removed from science consider what a preeminent chemist said about that.

The American Chemical Society (ACS) each year awards a gold medallion called the Priestly Medal to recognize distinguished services to chemistry. In 2007 the winner was George M. Whitesides and the ACS's journal, *Chemical & Engineering News* reported his address on that occasion. Regarding the origin of life, he said:

> This problem is one of the big ones in science. It begins to place life, and us, in the universe. Most chemists believe, as do I, that life emerged spontaneously from mixtures of molecules in the prebiotic Earth. How? I have no idea. Perhaps it was by the spontaneous emergence of "simple" autocatalytic cycles and then by their combination. On the basis of all the chemistry that I know, it seems to me astonishingly improbable. The idea of an RNA world is a good hint, but it is so far removed in its complexity from

dilute solutions of mixtures of simple molecules in a hot, reducing ocean under a high pressure of CO_2 that I don't know how to connect the two. We need a really good new idea. That idea would, of course, start us down the path toward systems that evolve autonomously—a revolution indeed.

That speech illustrates what Humanist scientists admit to each other and the problems with evolution that are discussed in the technical journals. However, the Humanist educational machine teaches children that evolution is settled science to which the *Catechism*'s authors refer us for the answers to life's most fundamental questions. For a more recent technical discussion about how impossible the origin of life from chemistry has been shown to be watch this
https://www.youtube.com/watch?v=Qte8NX4R8MY&t=746s

Source of the Information is the Achilles Heel
The effort that evolutionists make to fog up the question of life's origins, such as the PBS story "In Search of Life's Origins" reveals the well-known impasse in origin-of-life studies. In the Prologue to his 2013 *NYT* bestseller, *Darwin's Doubt*, Stephen Meyer explained:

> The type of information present in living cells—that is, "specified" information in which the sequence of characters matters to the function of the sequence as a whole—has generated an acute mystery. No undirected physical or chemical process has demonstrated the capacity to produce specified information starting "from purely physical or chemical" precursors. For this reason, chemical evolution theories have failed to solve the mystery of the origin of the first life—a claim that few mainstream evolutionary theorists now dispute.

Why Dr. Meyer wrote *Darwin's Doubt* is an interesting story in itself that he explained in its Prologue. He wrote that in his 2009 book, *Signature of the Cell*, he reported on the impasse (no explanation for the origin of first life) and argued the case for intelligent design. Although that book was limited to the origin of *first* life and the inadequacies of theories of chemical evolution that attempt to explain it, the book received a surprising response. Meyer said that "most criticized the book as if I had presented a critique of the standard neo- Darwinian theories of *biological* evolution." Most of his critics sought to refute his claim that no chemical evolutionary process had demonstrated the power to explain the *ultimate* origin of information in DNA (or RNA) necessary to produce life from simpler preexisting chemicals in the first place by citing processes at work in *already living organisms*. In other words, the responders touted the process of natural selection acting on random mutations in *already existing sections of information-rich DNA*. The critics proposed an undirected process that acts on preexisting information-rich DNA to refute Meyer's point that undirected material processes could not produce the information in DNA in the first place.

Humanists recognized that Meyer's logical conclusion for the ultimate cause of first life-- intelligence -- could unravel the whole evolutionary story. Meyer explained in *Darwin's Doubt* that he had long doubted that mutation and natural selection could add enough new information of the right kind to produce the large-scale changes supposed to have happened even after the origin of life in some form. However, for the sake of argument he had conceded that possibility. He said he found it "increasingly tedious" to concede the substance of arguments he thought were "likely to be false." The evolutionists criticism of arguments he did *not* make in *Signature of the Cell* motivated him to write the present book that responds to the supposed undirected evolution of living things from a common ancestor which is the story conveyed by textbooks, the popular media, and spokespersons for "official science."

What Was Darwin's Doubt?

Darwin's Doubt takes its title from something Darwin expressed in his famous work, *The Origin of Species*. Darwin was unable to explain in the light of his theories the fossil record which documented the sudden appearance of so many new and "anatomically sophisticated" creatures in the sedimentary layer called the Cambrian without any evidence of simpler ancestral forms. In other words, there were no ancestors and no transitional fossils in that sedimentary layer before the one called the Cambrian layer. Darwin wrote:

> The difficulty of understanding the absence of vast piles of fossiliferous strata, which on my theory were no doubt somewhere accumulated before the [Cambrian] epoch is very great …I allude to the manner in which the numbers of species of the same group suddenly appear in the lowest known fossiliferous rocks."

The sudden appearance of fully formed animals with no ancestors and no intermediate forms did not accord with his theory of gradual change. One might think that Darwin gained more conviction regarding his theory, especially as the years went by and he published six editions. However, far from being a definitive work, the *Origin* is saturated with conjecture. In the final 1876 printing of the 1872 sixth edition, Darwin employed the word "may" 642 times, "if" 493 times, "might" 203 times, "probable" or "probably" 182 times, "tend" or "tendency" 153 times, "suppose(d)" 141 times, "perhaps" 63 times, "no doubt" 58 times, "I believe" occurs 58 times, and "I think" 43 times, and so on.

World famous Jewish historian Gertrude Himmelfarb (d. 2019) in her 1959 classic *Darwin and the Darwinian Revolution* observed that far from constructing sound empirical arguments, Darwin usually engaged in rhetorical sleight-of-hand where "possibilities were promoted as probabilities, and probabilities into certainties, so ignorance itself was raised to a position once removed from certain knowledge." Yet in modern nations Darwin's disciples hold a belief in the fact of evolution with the zeal that only Humanist religion can inspire. That ought to give readers cause to reflect on why "evolution is a fact" is taught so zealously in spite of the lack of evidence.

Darwin's Doubt: The Explosion of Animal Life and the Case for Intelligent Design explores every theory of biological evolution by an extensive review of the books and papers published by evolutionary biologists. Meyer quotes them and shows why their theories can't explain the source of the information contained in living things. It is an enjoyable read. It is loaded with the latest natural science discoveries of which even serious students of the evolution controversy may not be aware. This is the book for any reader of my book who wants a really good technical explanation of all of the improbabilities of evolution that modern science has exposed. As one reviewer of Meyer's book noted:

> Darwinists keep two sets of books. The first set is the real record within peer-reviewed literature that discusses why the mechanism of the origin of life and the mode and tempo of speciation are more baffling today than they were two centuries ago. The second set of books is the popular literature that promotes to the public a soothing, fanciful narrative claiming that the grand history of life is fully explained with only minor but exciting details left to be filled in. Stephen Meyer [audits] the second set of books using the data found in the first.

Lipstick on a Corpse

The effort that was put into the PBS Evolution Project and the companion book *Evolution: The Triumph of An Idea* in 2000 reflects the desperate crisis in that 19th Century theory — almost like putting lipstick on a corpse. New discoveries by experimental scientists, not only in genetics but in other areas as well, have brought into question the evolutionary dogma. There is enormous disparity between popular representations of the status of the theory and its actual status as indicated in peer-reviewed technical journals. Dr. Meyer noted that

> Evolutionary biologists will acknowledge problems to each other in scientific settings that they will deny or minimize in public, lest they aid and abet the dreaded "creationists" and others they see as advancing the cause of unreason…It is an understandable, if ironic, human reaction, of course, but one that in the end deprives the public of access to what scientists actually know. It also perpetuates the impression of evolutionary biology as a science that has settled all the important questions at just the time when many new and exciting questions---about the origin of animal form, for example---are coming to the fore.

The Intelligent Design Movement

Biochemist Michael Denton, M.D., Ph.D., published *Evolution: A Theory in Crisis* in 1985. In it he presented a systematic critique of Neo-Darwinism ranging from paleontology, fossils, homology, molecular biology, genetics, and biochemistry. Dr. Denton made this prediction in that book:

> It would be an illusion to think that what we are aware of at present is any more than a fraction of the full extent of biological design. In practically every field of fundamental biological research ever-increasing levels of design and complexity are being revealed at an ever-increasing rate. The credibility of natural selection is weakened, therefore, not only by the perfection we have

already glimpsed but by the expectation of further as yet undreamt depths of ingenuity and complexity.

What Dr. Denton wrote in 1985 has certainly come to pass more than he imagined. Engineers have developed a whole new field called biophotonics, bringing light to the life sciences. As just one example, they have invented super-resolution microscopy that enables life science researchers to observe dynamic biological processes inside living cells with unprecedented clarity. Dr. Denton described himself as an agnostic who rejects biblical creationism. However, so impressive was his critique that it inspired what is now known as the Intelligent Design (ID) Movement which promotes the opposite view to Darwin's unguided random chance theories. The ID Movement is not informed by Divine Revelation and seems to concede geological naturalism if only for argument's sake. So, it is not in harmony with the Catholic doctrine of creation but it definitely contradicts Humanism's doctrine of biological naturalism. Dr Denton, even as a non-Christian outside observer to the creation/evolution debate, understood the centrality of *Genesis*:

> As far as Christianity was concerned, the advent of the theory of evolution and the elimination of traditional teleological thinking was catastrophic. The suggestion that life and man are the result of chance is incompatible with the biblical assertion of their being the direct result of intelligent creative activity. Despite the attempt by liberal theology to disguise the point, the fact is that no biblically derived religion can really be compromised with the fundamental assertion of Darwinian Theory. Chance and design are antithetical concepts, and the decline of religious belief can probably be attributed more to the propagation and advocacy by the intellectual and scientific community of the Darwinian version of evolution than to any other single factor.

Alienation of Catholic youth is taking place "under our noses" in schools every day and it takes a non-Christian to point it out. Also, atheist G.R.Bozarth, saw that clearly in 1978:

> Christianity has fought, still fights, and will fight science to the desperate end over evolution, because evolution destroys utterly and finally the very reason Jesus' earthly life was supposedly made necessary. Destroy Adam and Eve and the original sin, and in the rubble, you will find the sorry remains of the son of god. Take away the meaning of his death. If Jesus was not the redeemer who died for our sins, and this is what evolution means, then Christianity is nothing.
>
> (The Meaning of Evolution, *American Atheist* 20 (2):30)

Faith-Affirming Science

At the end of *Darwin's Doubt*, after he has explained why intelligent design is a scientific theory superior to the various variations of Darwinism, Stephen Meyer made this final point:

> The theory of intelligent design is not based on religious belief, nor does it provide a proof for the existence of God. But it does have faith-affirming implications precisely because it suggests the design we observe in the natural world is real, just as a traditional theistic view of the world would lead us to expect. Of course, that by itself is not a reason to accept the theory. But having accepted it for other reasons, it may be a reason to find it important.

In *Aquinas and Evolution*, Thomistic scholar Fr. Michael Chaberek observed that abstract philosophical arguments for the existence of God are

> more certain and permanent than scientific ones. Scientific arguments, however, are more concrete and easier to grasp for those who have not possessed the ability of abstract thinking. And this is why the persuasive

power of the scientific arguments for ID often turns out to be greater than the philosophical arguments for the existence of God. And this is why ID creates more resistance among unbelievers than any of the five ways [of proving God's existence] proposed by Aquinas.

Our Catholic youth can be taught the faith-affirming facts of natural science to counter the faith-destroying propaganda of the Humanists dogma of evolution. But it is a job that must be organized, led, and encouraged at the parish level. Can we get parish priests to facilitate the teaching of faith-affirming natural science? Or will they keep abjuring to their DREs who will keep doing conventional CCD that has failed for the last half century?

The Power of the Evolution Alliance

The evolution alliance comprised of schools, universities, and public and private institutions is too powerful for many parents to combat on their own. The power of the evolution alliance was well-illustrated by an incident in 2004. The editor of a biology journal, a man with a Ph. D. in evolutionary biology and systems biology, incurred a severe penalty for publishing an article that argued that intelligent design could help explain the origin of biological information. The journal was *Proceedings of the Biological Society of Washington* published by the Smithsonian Institution Museum of Natural History, a Federal Government facility whose employees are in the Federal Civil Service with all of the job protection rules that make it virtually impossible to fire anyone. The article provoked a national controversy. The evolutionist alliance was furious with Richard Sternberg for allowing the article to be peer-reviewed and publishing it. Museum officials removed him from office and transferred him to a hostile supervisor. They tried to get him to resign but when that failed, they demoted him. Yet, the offending article itself drew no rebuttal because of the typical dodge evolutionists use to

73

avoid debate: they didn't want to dignify it by responding. Humanists control the popular media, the science journals, the research grants, the universities, and the public schools. Professor Rodney Stark, preeminent American sociologist of religion, observed in *Scientific American* that: "There's been 200 years of marketing that if you want to be a scientific person you've got to keep your mind free of the fetters of religion." He further notes that in research universities "the religious people keep their mouths shut," while "irreligious people discriminate." According to Stark, "there's a reward system to being irreligious in the upper echelons [of the scientific community]."

Teachers and grant-dependent research scientists who want to remain employed must follow the party line. The lesson taught to Richard Sternberg was not lost on them. That is why authentic natural science education at the parish level is necessary. No scientific expertise is necessary to utilize the great tools and resources available, many at no cost. For example, see Appendix III of this book.

Science Education Powerhouse
The ID Movement is led by the Discovery Institute's Center for Science and Culture founded in 1990 and based in Seattle. It was inspired by Dr. Denton's book. The Discovery Institute is highly active in many areas. Lots of free information.
http://www.discovery.org/id/

ID and the Evolutionist Cardinal
Evolutionist Christoph Schönborn, Archbishop of Vienna, had an Op-Ed in the *NY Times* on July 7, 2005 defending ID. Also, in his book, *Chance or Purpose?* (Ignatius Press, 2007), Schönborn opined that while it is legitimate for those doing research "along strictly scientific methodological lines" to exclude the search for purpose, or finality, from their way of studying nature, it is

illegitimate and, indeed, irrational for them to conclude from their findings that there is no purpose, or finality, in the world of nature. And so, he reasoned that the aggressive manner in which many working scientists have opposed the group of American scientists who are searching for more evidences of intelligent design in the natural world "does not have much to do with science."

In his review of Schönborn's book, Msgr. John F. McCarthy, J.C.D., S.T.D. wrote that the book is an effort to show how the biological evolution of the human body fits in with the divine plan for man. "The Cardinal clearly presents the viewpoint of a theistic evolutionist, but it is odd that he accepts so confidently Darwin's claim of the descent of man from lower animals while, at the same time, admitting that, concerning the validity of the theory of evolution, 'so many questions still remain open.'"

Theistic Evolutionists Are Vague About Details

Theistic evolutionists agree that macroevolution happened through mutations and natural selection (Darwinism) acting through the laws of nature that God established when He created whatever it was that He created. As Stephen Meyer showed in *Darwin's Doubt*, mutation and natural selection could not add enough new specified information of the right kind to produce the large-scale changes supposed to have happened even after the origin of life in some form. Further, as related earlier, empirical scientists such as John Sanford and Daniel Lieberman testify that mutations remove information from the human genome and are harmful. Theistic and atheistic evolution are functionally identical. The only distinction is the empty theological language attached in the former case.

Chapter 5- Noah and Evolutionary Geology

Evolutionary theory is incompatible with any sort of a world-wide flood as described in *Genesis*. Evolutionary theory requires a very ancient earth. The theory that the earth is very ancient depends on the uniformitarian theory of geology.

Humanist philosophy harkens back to the ancient Greek philosophers. Many of those believed in evolution and a very old Earth. Therefore, Noah's flood had always been a stumbling block to the spread of Humanist philosophy. It was a supernatural event and a marker in the *Genesis* chronology that gave an approximate age to the Earth. If there was no such flood, then the "wear and tear" was caused by presently observed natural causes and for such natural causes to have done that much "wear and tear" would have taken billions of years according to uniformitarian geology. How uniformitarian geology became the scientific consensus and paved the way for Darwinian evolution theory is explained in this chapter.

One aim of the Enlightenment was to challenge the authority of beliefs inherited from Christian culture. In that atmosphere, alongside of true empirical science, there developed a new genre, "pre-historical science," that included observation, data collection, naturalistic hypotheses regarding the data, and logical reasoning. Inferences could be drawn, but conclusions could not be proved or disproved, and they lacked predictive value.

In an earlier chapter you read that in the 18th Century Kant and Laplace combined on the nebular theory that the Earth formed itself from dust and gas. Scotsman James Hutton, in 1788, published his *Theory of the Earth* in which he proposed the explanation of how Earth's geology had developed. Humanists embraced and propagated that pre-historic geology hypotheses that was compatible with naturalism.

Except for two years studying medicine in France and the Netherlands, Hutton never left Scotland; yet he proposed a theory that encompassed the world. From his visit to Siccar Point in Scotland, he concluded that the rocks forming the Earth were formed in fire by volcanic activity, with a continuing gradual process of weathering and erosion wearing away rocks, which were then deposited on the sea bed, re-formed into layers of sedimentary rock by heat and pressure, and raised again. For the features on the Earth to have formed in that manner required a long, long time. On that hypothesis, geologic or deep time was invented and the atheists' modern theory that the Earth is billions of years old advanced.

Hutton was not a scientist. He was a part of the "Scottish Enlightenment" and associated with its famous Humanist philosophers, such as David Hume. Hutton's theory was slow to catch on, but it was embraced by Humanists because it was a naturalistic alternative to Noah's supernatural flood. Hutton's theory provided the vast ages of time that evolutionists invest with creative power. Hutton's theory is known as Uniformitarianism. The theory assumes that the same natural laws and processes that operate in the universe now have always operated in the universe in the past and apply everywhere in the universe. It has included the gradualistic concept that "the present is the key to the past," and is functioning at the same rates. According to his hypothesis, the history of the Earth could be determined by understanding how processes such as volcanism, erosion, and sedimentation work in the present day.

In the next century, Charles Lyell, a trained lawyer, was studying geology and heard lectures by the Protestant clergyman and geologist William Buckland who, at that point in his career, was opposing Hutton's theories. In 1820 Buckland published *Connexion of Geology with Religion explained,* both justifying the new science of geology and reconciling geological evidence with the biblical accounts of creation and Noah's Flood. This theory was Catastrophism. But Hutton's theories kept gaining acceptance in Humanist philosophy circles.

Lyell and Darwin

Charles Lyell took up Hutton's ideas, expanded them, and popularized his theoretical framework in an 1830 book, *Principles of Geology: being an attempt to explain the former changes to the Earth's surface, by reference to causes now in operation.* Lyell's hypothesis, the opposite of the then-consensus belief in Catastrophism, caught on immediately in the swelling ranks of Humanism because it also explained away a supernatural event like Noah's flood and provided a naturalistic hypothesis to assign a vast age to the Earth. Nearly everything Lyell speculated about was accepted by Humanist opinion makers because, as Darwin recognized before he published his famous book in 1859, evolutionary theories of biology depend on timescales so long that almost anything can be proposed without possibility of disproof. Paradoxically though, evolution cannot be proved by any "causes now in operation," which is the working principle of evolutionary geology.

Charles Lyell is the one who arranged for divinity student and amateur biologist Charles Darwin's passage on the British Navy ship that took him to the Western Hemisphere, where he developed the basics of his theory. Darwin took Lyell's book with him and made observations through the lens of Lyell's vast ages.

Gould: Deep Time Not Based on Evidence

Lyell's contribution to the acceptance of "deep-time geology" and to biological evolution was not the work of science one would think it was based on its quick acceptance. Evolutionist Harvard professor Stephen Jay Gould ranked the development of the "deep time" concept as important as the developments associated with Copernicus and Darwin. But in his 1987 book, *Time's Arrow Time's Cycle: Myth and metaphor in the discovery of geological time,* Gould observed that Lyell was rewriting geological history … the reconstructed historical narrative that Lyell wanted to portray was that Hutton's gradual processes were accepted based on empirical evidence against the untested theories of the catastrophists. Gould suggests this was "one of the most flagrant mischaracterizations ever perpetrated by the heroic tradition in the history of science."

In other words, it was not the *evidence* that set the age at billions of years, but rather the *interpretation* of the observations of data and its subsequent popularization which turned it into an axiom. The interpretation that features of the Earth require a long, long time to form was "exploded" by the evidence from the 1980 explosion of Mt. St. Helens in the state of Washington.
https://creation.com/lessons-from-mount-st-helens
But facts like that, if made known, would spoil the evolutionary tale.

The Debate Hinges on This

Determining whether Noah's flood took place as described in the Bible or not is the key to understanding the whole debate about evolution which ascribes creative power to time. It perhaps explains why *The Genesis Flood* (published 1961) had such an impact on those who read it. It included observed data about the earth that only make sense when explained by a cataclysmic world-wide flood. Among other things, *The Genesis Flood* documented plenty of scientific data that indicate we live on a young Earth and not one that is 4.5 billion years old. Evolutionists never mention this data and they do not mention the assumptions upon which their "ancient earth" estimates depend. As one example, consider the magnetic field of the earth. The magnetic field is a shield essential for our survival because it deflects destructive cosmic radiation from space around the Earth. It has been measured repeatedly since 1829 and the data, when plotted on a graph, show the strength of the field has decreased and is decaying exponentially. If as uniformitarian geology maintains, the present is the key to the past, then that data can be extrapolated backwards. Extrapolating 10,000 years backward on that exponential curve indicates the magnetic field would be so strong that the Earth would be uninhabitable. That would indicate the Earth is young as the Bible teaches. The solution to that problem offered by evolutionists, because they "know" the Earth is billions of years old, is that the magnetic field reversed itself many times over the course of Earth's history. How, when, and why these reversals happened has remained in the realm of naturalistic speculation. Whether or not there have been reversals in Earth's magnetic field is a matter for further debate and investigation, but if reversals have occurred, they most likely occurred rapidly over a very short time period during a major Earth-wide catastrophe such as the Flood. For more on the magnetic field see https://www.icr.org/article/earths-young-magnetic-field/

New Data Shake Up 100-Year-Old Hypothesis

Discover is an evolutionary science magazine. According to an article in the July-August 2014 issue, "Journeys to the Center of the Earth," scientists claim to know that Earth's magnetic field is caused by the slow, convective, sloshing of liquid iron in the Earth's outer core (estimated to be 1800 miles below the surface), aided by Earth's rotation. That is the "geodynamo hypothesis" that originated in 1919 but proving it is yet beyond the reach of any theory, computer simulation, or experiment in the 100+ years since. See more on that here https://creation.com/moons-magnetic-puzzle

According to the *Discover* article, "Evidence from ancient rocks reveals that Earth's geodynamo has been running for at least 3.5 billion years." *Discover* continued:

> Two years ago, a team of scientists from two British universities discovered that liquid iron, at the temperatures and pressures found [according to theory] in the outer core, conducts far more heat into the mantle than anyone had thought possible...This discovery is vexing. If liquid iron conducts heat into the mantle at such a high rate, there wouldn't be enough heat left in the outer core to churn its ocean of iron liquid. In other words, there would be no heat-driven convection in the outer core. "This is a big problem," says Alfe [the lead researcher] "because convection is what drives the geodynamo. We would not have a geodynamo without convection."

The article went on to say that a team in Japan validated the British team's result regarding the heat transfer properties of iron at high pressure. The article continued:

> Based on how fast Earth's core is cooling and solidifying now, it's likely that the inner core formed relatively recently, perhaps within the past billion years. How did the geodynamo manage to function for at least a couple of billion years before the inner core existed? "The problem is actually in Earth's past," not in the present says Alfe. "This is where new hypotheses are coming in. Some people are saying maybe Earth was a lot hotter in the past."

Also, in 2018 the technical journal *Earth and Planetary Science Letters* published an article asserting that technically, the Earth's inner core should not exist. https://www.livescience.com/61715-earth-inner-core-paradox.html

Another geologic "fact" that every school child learns is that the various continents are the result of land mass shifts caused by the movement of tectonic plates over millions of years. Plate tectonics was introduced in the early 1960s and was quickly adopted by most geologists. Despite widespread acceptance, it remains essentially unchanged and continues to include nagging, unresolved problems. The cataclysmic Noah's Flood explains the Earth's geology better than the slow movement of plates.

Fossil Fuel from Buried Once-Living Material
Fossil fuel is a general term for buried combustible geologic deposits of organic (derived from living matter) materials that have been converted to crude oil, coal, natural gas, or heavy oils by exposure to heat and pressure in the earth's crust. According to evolutionists this happened over hundreds of millions of years. When Hutton and Lyell were sitting in Great Britain centuries ago and writing the geologic history of the world under candles or a lamp burning whale oil, did they ever imagine that vast reservoirs of crude oil, natural gas, and coal would be found from Pole to Pole on land and under the oceans thousands of feet below the surface? How, one wonders, would they account for the massive and deep burial of the organic material by the gradualism theory they proposed?

In Wyoming there are coal seams 200 feet high. At least 6 seams are over 100 feet high and some run for up to 75 miles. Those coal seams were deposited during the Flood as flood waters receded, trapping trillions of tons of plant-rich debris in mats between sediments in the subsiding Powder River Basin. The

June 15, 2019 edition of the *Journal of Asian Earth Sciences* described coal beds 175 miles off the coast of Borneo that are 5,000 feet thick, cover 3800 square miles and are 1.9 miles below sea level. Oil rigs have drilled wells 35,000 feet into the ocean floor. For more information on the formation of fossil fuel watch https://www.youtube.com/watch?v=r3K9HG6BfaA

Since the mid-19th Century Humanists and other proponents of evolutionary geology have been repeating that "the present is the key to the past." Earthquakes, volcanoes, sedimentation, and erosion of the type happening in any period of history did not clump those trillions and trillions of tons of plants, trees, marine algae, and animals together and rapidly bury them below the surface in pockets and seams found everywhere on earth. And it doesn't take millions of years to make fossil fuel. Crude oil can be made from marine algae in an hour. See
http://creation.com/algae-to-oil

What do you know about Noah's Flood?
Those with superficial knowledge of *Genesis* 6-8 say "Oh, I know, it rained for 40 days and nights." What *Genesis* 7:11 says is that "all the fountains of the great deep burst forth and the windows of the heavens were opened." Most of the water came from underground. Even today there is more water in the earth's mantle than in its oceans. https://www.icr.org/article/oceans-water-deep-beneath-earth/ It was a cataclysmic event that took 150 days to cover the mountains and about 7 months to drain off. Noah was in the Ark for 371 days.

Arctic Fossils, Antarctic Rainforest
The Genesis Flood is a source for all sort of evidence for a world-wide catastrophic flood as described by Moses. In 1961 that book described how buried in the Arctic regions there is vast evidence that before the Flood that area of the world was no colder than

elsewhere because it contains so many fossils of animals and flora now found only in temperate and tropical regions. The evolutionists also know the Arctic was once warm and wonder why because they reject the Flood. The April 2015 issue of *Discover* magazine contained an article titled "Cold Case: Is our climate's future written in Arctic fossils from a warmer past?" The article is about a Canadian paleobiologist named Rybczynski "looking for clues about past global warming" in a period, according to evolutionary dating, "3 to 3.3 million years ago." This contradicts the current Humanist hysterical claim that humans cause "global warming."

> Today Ellesmere [Island], which lies next to Greenland on the eastern edge of Canada's Arctic Archipelago, supports only ankle-high tufts of cotton grass and mossy ground cover; the nearest tree is almost 1000 miles south. But Rybczynski and her colleagues have unearthed evidence of a balmier Arctic from a time referred to as the mid-Pliocene warm period, roughly 3 million to 3.3 million years ago. The Island's treasure trove of fossils, preserved in permafrost suggests the area was once an ancient boreal-like forest of larch cedar and birch grazed by miniature beavers, three-toed horses, and bear ancestors.

The article went on to explain that Rybczynski had once found a bone in that Arctic wasteland that was later identified as the tibia bone of a camel that was 30% larger than that of a modern camel. Ironically, the identification was made possible because of collagen in the bone. Collagen is a tough structural protein that ties or connects other tissues such as skin and bones. Since this material should have completely decomposed after only thousands of years, none should be left after the millions of years assigned to these remains. An evolutionist colleague of Rybczynski named Ballantyne was puzzled by these findings regarding the forests that once were there.

For a productive forest to grow, Ballantyne explains, temperatures have to remain above freezing for half the year…Three distinct data sets pointed to the same number: an average yearly temperature 34 F warmer than today's Arctic…While average global temperatures in the mid-Pliocene rose only 3.6 to 5.4F, the Arctic was a totally different world. "So the question is what was amplifying temperatures in the Arctic?" Ballantyne asks.

Smithsonian, April 2016, included testimony from the director of the National Museum of Natural History. Kirk Johnson spent two summers on Ellesmere Island. "We were finding fossils from a much warmer world. We found a rhinoceros skeleton on an unnamed river, so we named it—it's the only Rhinoceros River in Canada. We found petrified forests and crocodiles and turtles and early mammals." Articles published in the *Bulletin of Canadian Petroleum Geology* in 1982 and 1987 reported fossils found in the Eureka Sound Group in Northwest Canada—e.g., lemurs, alligators, turtles, and swamp cypress—indicate the paleoclimate ranged from tropical to warm temperate with little seasonal contrast (equable).

An article, "Polar Opposites," in the April 2, 2020 issue of *Nature* described the bafflement of scientists who found evidence that a rainforest once grew in Antarctica based on core samples of sediment taken in 2017. According to an April 1st post on CNN.com, study co-author and Imperial College London professor Tina van de Flierdt said"

The preservation of this 90-million-year-old forest is exceptional, but even more surprising is the world it reveals… Even during months of darkness, swampy temperate rainforests were able to grow … revealing an even warmer climate than we expected.

The Mist Canopy Hypothesis

Why were the Arctic and Antarctic warm at one time and supported forests and animals where there is now a desert of ice? One hypothesis is based on *Genesis* 1: 6-7:

> And God said, 'Let there be firmament in the midst of the waters, and let it separate the waters from the waters. And God made the firmament and separated the waters which were under the firmament from the waters that were above the firmament." And it was so.

Translation of the Hebrew word *raqiya* went to Greek to Latin to English to become "firmament" but the latest research translates it as "expanse," that is, the space around the Earth. Picture the Earth as we now know it, surrounded by air which becomes thinner with the height above the Earth. The main protection for the Earth from the harmful cosmic radiation from the sun and other bodies in space is the magnetic field and the ozone layer. But, if at the Creation, beyond that air, instead of the empty, airless vacuum of space there was a canopy of water mist, what would be the effect? The answer is a green house effect. The rays of heat-bearing light coming toward Earth would hit that water mist and be spread around the Earth so that instead of the Equatorial Region being hot and the North and South Poles being cold, the whole Earth would be temperate. The Earth's mild climate would enable the growth everywhere of the lush vegetation necessary to support large populations of people, plants, and animals, even for vast consumers like dinosaurs.

If there was a water mist canopy as that hypothesis proposes, what happened to it? *Genesis* 7:11 says that "all the fountains of the great deep burst forth and the windows of the heavens were opened." What were those "windows of heaven" that opened? There is no mist up there now. I am not suggesting that the mist (if it was there) was the source of the 40 days of rain and a major cause of the flooding. Scientific modeling has ruled out that amount of water in the theoretical canopy because the "greenhouse" would have been too hot. But God may have "fine-tuned" the amount of mist and its distance from Earth to fulfill His purpose. Anyone who doesn't know about God's "fine tuning" should read books by secular scientists such as *A Fortunate Universe: Life in a Finely Tuned Cosmos* (2016), *Rare Earth: Why Complex Life is Uncommon in the Universe* (2000) or *The Privileged Planet: How Our Place in the Cosmos Is Designed for Discovery* (2004). A fine-tuned mist is only a hypothesis that could never be proved but it may explain why the Arctic was once warm. A quick read about God's "fine tuning" is https://creation.com/the-universe-is-finely-tuned-for-life .

A Digression: Fine Tuning and the Atheists

A great summary of the fine tuning discovered by physicists that has turned many atheists into theists is in Stephen Meyer's *The Return of the God Hypothesis: Three Scientific Discoveries That Reveal The Mind Behind The Universe* (HarperCollins paperback edition, 2023.) Sir Fred Hoyle, who with his "Steady State Model," had fought so hard to prove that the universe had always existed, contributed enormously to the fine-tuning discoveries. Since he believed that "we came from the stars," so to speak, he puzzled over the mysterious presence of so much carbon in the universe. How, he wondered, might have relatively "heavy" carbon formed inside the stars which through nuclear fusion produce "light" elements such as hydrogen and helium. According to Meyer:

> Hoyle was stunned by these and other "cosmic coincidences" that physicists began to discover after the 1950s. Whereas he affirmed atheism and denied any evidence of design, he began to see fine tuning as obvious evidence of intelligent design.

87

In the November 1981 issue of *Engineering & Science* Hoyle wrote that

> A common- sense interpretation of the facts suggests that a super-intellect has monkeyed with physics, as well as with chemistry and biology, and that there are no blind forces worth speaking about in nature. The numbers one calculates from the facts seems to me so overwhelming as to put this conclusion beyond question.

Back to the Flood

If most of the water for the Flood did not come down, did it come up? When "all the fountains of the great deep burst forth," water above the crust of the Earth and much more below may have created massive fountains spurting miles into the sky with enormous pressure to create the "rain." There is a crack that goes all the way around the Earth under the oceans and on a topographic map it looks like the seams on a baseball. The seafloor is dotted with thousands of steep-sided underwater volcanoes, or seamounts. The world's largest volcano, Pūhāhonu, is 700 miles northwest of Hawaii and almost completely submerged beneath the Pacific Ocean. In 2004 a tsunami from just one underwater earthquake in the Indian Ocean killed 250,000 people. Imagine the terror when the "fountains of the great deep burst forth."

The scaring of the Earth, its jagged mountains with marine fossils on top of them, the wasteland deserts, the trillions and trillions of tons of deeply buried plants and animals that became fossil fuel, the massive fossil grave yards such as over 1000 fossilized whales in the desert 150 km southwest of Cairo all point to a catastrophic Flood. See https://creation.com/fossil-graveyard-points-to-catastrophic-demise

The Flood and the Dinosaurs

According to evolutionists at the Smithsonian Institution:

> Sixty-five million years ago the dinosaurs died out along with more than 50% of other life forms on the planet. This mass extinction is so dramatic that for many years it was used to mark the boundary between the Cretaceous Period, when the last dinosaurs lived, and the Tertiary Period, when no dinosaurs remained.

That story is repeated everywhere in the textbooks and culture as if it were a fact. It contains several evolutionary assumptions and circular reasoning. The Cretaceous Period just means the water-borne sedimentary deposit layer on some parts of the Earth's crust that evolutionists, following the Hutton-Lyle theory of Earth's formation, say was laid down 65 million years ago. They date it at 65 million years because that is the layer in which most buried dinosaurs are found and dinosaurs are said to have died 65 million years ago. This is an example of fossil-rock dating circular reasoning that teachers never explain to students. An Australian secondary school teacher contributed an article to *Creation* magazine (Oct. 2012) that may help readers understand fossil-rock dating based on index fossils:

> Evolutionary paleontologists use 'index fossils' to assign an age to a layer of sedimentary rock and its associated fossils. Evolutionary theory assumes that a particular creature evolved from its ancestors, lived successfully for a period, then became extinct as its descendants evolved better ways of surviving. In other words, that creature had a defined 'evolutionary life-span'. We may be told, "It thrived in the Devonian period." For example, we all 'know' that the dinosaurs 'evolved' about 230 million years ago, and died out 65 million years ago, don't we? Or do we? To 'know' that, people need to make two assumptions. One is that fossils and rocks can be assigned

an 'age' directly, through various scientific techniques [e.g., radiometric]. However, no matter how accurate the measurements of chemicals in the rocks are, there is no way of calibrating a dating technique for supposedly pre-historic events. Despite paleontologists trying to make sense of these scientific measures, the 'dates' they assign to rocks are constrained by the fossils found in them. For example, if dinosaur fossils are found in a rock layer, the rocks are *assumed* to be at least 65 million years old. So, if a radiometric dating [itself full of assumptions] result indicates an age of 40 million years, it is interpreted as representing, not the age of the rock, but a later geological process, such as disturbance, reworking or contamination. The fossils always trump the supposedly objective radiometric dating!

The second assumption has two complementary parts. First, in the strata above and below ("after and before") the range where fossils of a particular creature are known, it is assumed it didn't exist *at that time*. Evolutionists would say either that it hadn't evolved yet, or that it had become extinct. Second and conversely, if a particular fossil is frequently found in rocks of a particular 'age' then we can say that that creature is an indicator fossil for rocks of that age—an 'index fossil.' In other words, rocks that contain fossils of that creature must be of that 'age, and so must any associated fossils.

But can we be sure that, if a creature does not appear in the fossil record of a particular age range of rocks, it did not exist then? No, we can't. Consider the many so-called 'living fossils'—creatures whose fossils are not found in any rocks younger [according to evolutionary dating] than a certain age, but discovered alive today. One famous example is the coelacanth, a fish regarded as becoming extinct supposedly 65 million years ago because it was missing from the fossil record since then. Yet, in 1938, it was discovered to be still alive. Similarly, the recent discoveries in the last two decades of dinosaur bones that contained tissue that was still flexible, as well as blood cells, challenges the idea that dinosaurs disappeared from the earth 65 million years ago. [Because flexible material and blood cells couldn't possibly last that long.]

Readers are encouraged to look at this very short video about that discovery. https://www.youtube.com/watch?v=XEtL6XjRqMg

The lab scientist who first discovered flexible tissue and blood cells in "65-million-year-old" dinosaur bones first published in the 1990s. She found similar results on two more different dinosaurs and her 2009 publication in *Science*, May 2009 drew enough attention that she was featured on the TV program "60 minutes." A 3-minute clip from that program must be watched not only to show the discovery is real operational science but also to hear the reaction from the "scientific consensus" to it. https://www.youtube.com/watch?v=0-K7_H27Wq4

The proteins identified included type I collagen, elastin, actin, tropomyosin, and hemoglobin, like proteins in vertebrates alive today. Discovery of still-soft tissue and cellular structures in dinosaur bones is, despite the evidence, "controversial" because it challenges conventional wisdom that dinosaurs became extinct 65 million years ago and no mechanisms have been identified that could reasonably contribute to such preservation. Calculations from today's chemistry show that the proteins should have disintegrated and disappeared long, long ago and no mechanism is known to prevent that. Despite the evidence that continues to accumulate of intact proteins in dinosaur fossils, "skepticism" persists because evolutionists so want it to be true that dinosaurs lived millions and millions of years ago.

Mass Extinction in Genesis Flood?

The sudden, mass extinction is entirely consistent with a catastrophic flood. Although baby dinosaurs would have been on Noah's Ark, they, and the more than 50% of other life forms on the planet that evolutionists say suddenly became extinct, would have had difficulty foraging on the recently denuded planet. The current "scientific consensus," which denies there was the Flood, has wrestled with the "mystery." Naturally, such a mystery as dinosaur extinction has spawned a wide range of theories, ranging from the plausible to the entertaining. In 1963, a geologist counted 46 theories, and many more have been added since then. The mystery is heightened when one realizes that the dinosaurs were well adapted to their environments and apparently had a worldwide distribution. Dinosaurs have been unearthed on every continent, including Antarctica. *Smithsonian*'s May 2018 cover story was "China's Dinosaur Boom" about the enormous numbers being found. Their traces are even found on a few isolated oceanic islands, such as Spitsbergen in the North Atlantic and North Island, New Zealand. Dinosaur tracks have been discovered at over 1,500 locations around the world. Tracks are even known from polar latitudes, such as in Alaska near the coast of the Arctic Ocean. Some areas display tracks on multiple layers of sedimentary rock. Dinosaur eggs, as well as nests, embryos, and hatchlings, have been discovered in nearly 200 locations. Millions of fossilized dinosaur eggs (or parts thereof) have been found. Dinosaur eggs are hard to identify to a particular parent species but fossilized embryos discovered both inside and outside of the egg have enabled paleontologists to do that. For example, thousands of titanosaur eggs, some with embryos and scaly skin, have been found in Auca Mahuevo, Argentina. The discovery of eggs and embryos preserved all around the world indicates rapid burial in lots of sediment. That is strong evidence of the catastrophic global *Genesis* Flood. So, what does the current evolutionist "scientific consensus" say happened to the dinosaurs if there was no catastrophic Flood?

On April 10, 2019 there was an editorial in *Nature*, "Why we can't get over the death of the dinosaurs: Reports of a new-found snapshot of extinction highlights a mystery that scientists are still working to solve." That editorial was provoked by a typical popular magazine sensationalizing a published research paper and turning it into "the smoking gun" proof for something or other about which professionals are still arguing. In this case, it was the March 29, 2019 issue of *The New Yorker* which published "The Day the Dinosaurs Died: A young paleontologist may have discovered a record of the most significant event in the history of life on Earth." The sensational headline is superimposed on a photograph that looks like something out of an Indiana Jones movie. If you've ever seen Harrison Ford as Indiana Jones, you'll recognize *The New Yorker*'s effort to glamorize a graduate student from the University of Kansas. https://www.newyorker.com/magazine/2019/04/08/the-day-the-dinosaurs-died

The New Yorker's "young paleontologist" photographed dressed as Indy is just the lead author, with 11 co-authors, of a paper titled "A seismically induced onshore surge deposit at the KPg boundary, North Dakota" published in *Proceedings of the National Academy of Science*. The team named their dig site "Tanis." Regarding the overreaction and sensationalism by *The New Yorker*, the editorial in *Nature* said:

> Others were more cautious. Paleontologists pushed back on social media and in news stories, noting many of the claims in *The New Yorker* article have yet to be assessed and verified. And the fact that the team named the site Tanis, after the ancient Egyptian city depicted in the 1981

film *Raiders of the Lost Ark*, caused more than a few eyes to roll.

The hero of the *New Yorker* magazine article, Robert DePalma, was "busted" for probable scientific fraud in December 2022 in connection with his dino-killing paper.

Paleontologist accused of faking data in dino-killing asteroid paper | Science | AAAS

The Great Asteroid Theory

An example of the more cautious approach was an article in *Science* on April 1, 2019, "Astonishment, skepticism greet fossils claimed to record dinosaur-killing asteroid impact." The "dinosaur-killing asteroid impact" mentioned in the title of the *Science* article is the current favorite among the bizarre stories the evolutionists have cooked up to explain the sudden extinction of dinosaurs. That story is that a gigantic asteroid hit the Earth at a site known as Chicxulub Crater on the Yucatán peninsula in south-east Mexico. The theory proposed by the geologist Walter Alvarez in about 1980 is that a meteor strike 66.4 million years ago caused dramatic climatic changes much like 'nuclear winter'. This, he theorized, caused the extinction of the dinosaurs and many other species. His evidence was his discovery of an allegedly world-wide layer of clay with a high iridium content. (Iridium is rare on Earth but plentiful on meteorites but subsequent research has found very little iridium at the Crater. www.icr.org/article/chicxulub-crater-theory-mostly-smoke/)

His father Luis, who won the Nobel Prize in Physics in 1968 for work on subatomic particles, helped him publicize the theory. It is now accepted as 'proven fact' in many circles, and popularized in 'documentaries' such as *Walking with Dinosaurs*. For example, the April 10, 2019 editorial in *Nature* mentioned above began as follows:

Sixty-six million years ago, an enormous asteroid slammed into Mexico's Yucatan peninsula, triggering a mass extinction that killed every dinosaur except the ancestor of birds.

Nature's editorial writer felt no need to explains why the only dinosaurs that didn't die were "the ancestors of birds." But it must be "true" because, according one theory taught as fact, birds evolved from dinosaurs later so there had to have been dinosaurs that survived so that birds could evolve. Perhaps unknown to that editorial writer is that among evolutionists who specialize in "bird evolution" there is a fight carried out in the technical journals about that. The "dino-bird" faction is led by Ucal Berkley's Kevin Padian. The other faction, led by North Carolina University's Alan Feduccia, maintain that birds evolved from a very different group of extinct reptiles. The claims and counter-claims of the two factions are described in Jonathan Well's *Zombie Science*.

The Great Volcanic Theory

The theory most competitive to the "Great Asteroid Theory" is the "Great Volcanic Theory." *Nature*, December 16, 2008 published "Volcanoes implicated in death of dinosaurs: Groups argue that an impact wasn't to blame."

Three research groups have released evidence suggesting that the dinosaurs were wiped out 65 million years ago by massive volcanic eruptions in India, rather than a meteorite impact as most scientists have thought. The research, based on samples from drilling in India, shows that four large eruptions coincided with the Cretaceous/Tertiary (K/T) event, which killed off a large fraction of life on land and in the seas.

The "Volcanic Theory" is alive and well. For example, on February 22, 2019 *Science* published "The eruptive tempo of

Deccan volcanism in relation to the Cretaceous-Paleogene boundary." As described by the editorial in *Nature*, that article featured "two extraordinarily precise studies of the timing of the eruptions" in India "and the Chicxulub impact leave open the question of whether volcanoes and the asteroid worked in a one-two punch to wipe out life on Earth." About a month later *The New Yorker* was "breaking news" about the discovery of "the "Day the Dinosaurs Died" because of an asteroid. This is a classic example of the way popular literature promotes to the public a soothing, fanciful narrative claiming that the grand history of life is fully explained with only minor but exciting details left to be filled in.

All secular theories for the extinction of dinosaurs face numerous problems, including the Chicxulub asteroid and volcanic eruptions in India theories. For example, if an asteroid hit the earth leading to a nuclear winter, how did the photosynthesis-dependent plants survive? Why did delicate bees and butterflies, or even sensitive amphibians such as frogs and salamanders survive? If volcanic activity and toxic gases filled the earth after an extinction event (such as the volcanic or carbon dioxide theory of extinction), then why did the birds survive?

Do Evolutionist Theories Explain the Mass Burials?
The two principal theories of the evolutionists, the Asteroid Theory, and the Volcanic Theory, involve the creation of large dust clouds that supposedly caused a change in the weather by blocking out the sun's warmth to such an extent that the dinosaurs perished. If dinosaurs died in such a scenario, one would expect them to be peeled off individually and for their carcasses to rot on the surface and disappear. Instead, throughout the world, we find these big, formidable animals buried and often clumped together. For example, at Dinosaur National Monument on the Colorado/Utah border, one can visit the Quarry Exhibit

Hall which exposes a sedimentary deposit in which a variety of dinosaurs were rapidly buried and their bones fossilized. According to the National Park Service:

> The Quarry Exhibit Hall allows visitors to view the wall of approximately 1,500 dinosaur bones in a refurbished, comfortable space. Here, you can gaze upon the remains of numerous different species of dinosaurs including *Allosaurus, Apatosaurus, Camarasaurus, Diplodocus,* and *Stegosaurus* along with several others

For more about the competing evolutionary stories about the demise of the dinosaurs and why their death from a global flood is indicated, see creation.com/the-extinction-of-the-dinosaurs. For more information about the Hell Creek Formation see www.icr.org/article/marine-fossils-mixed-hell-creek-dinosaurs/

The Flood Even Buried Most Sharks

An article in *Science,* June 4, 2021, "An early Miocene extinction in pelagic sharks" reports research on the "Mysterious Mass Extinction." According to the research paper's abstract:

> Studying shark teeth buried in deep sea sediment, Sibert and Rubin reveal that current shark diversity is a small remnant of a much larger array of forms that were decimated by a previously unidentified major ocean extinction event. The extinction led to a reduction in shark diversity by more than 70% and an almost complete loss in total abundance. There is no known climatic and/or environmental driver of this extinction, and its cause remains a mystery.

On April 29, 2022 *USA Today's* article "'Fish lizard' fossils found in Swiss Alps showcase some of the largest creatures to ever live" summarized a report in the *Journal of Vertebrate Paleontology* about the discovery high in the Swiss Alps of marine reptile carnivores, known as ichthyosaurs. "They were some the largest creatures to ever live on Earth – even bigger than sperm whales and on par with dinosaurs – given that they weighed about 80 tons and spanned 65 feet." There are fossils of marine creatures in limestone near the summit of Mt. Everest and other mountains such as the Canadian Rockies. Those show that those areas must have been under the sea in the past.

Many people would not associate the limestone and fossils on Everest with Noah's Flood because they think there was not enough water to cover the highest mountains. However, according to *Psalm 104:6-9*, the Flood changed the earth's topography. The mountains rose and the valleys sank down at the end of the Flood. With vertical earth movements towards the end of the Flood, the mountains rose and the water flowed off the continents into the newly formed oceans' basins. That's one explanation for why there are marine fossils at the tops of high mountains. The ocean basins cover 71% of the total area of the Earth and contain enough water to cover the whole planet to a depth of 2.7 km (1.7 miles) if the surface were completely flat.

The Pope Who Authoritatively Taught about Noah's Flood

If this writer has not succeeded in communicating to theistic evolutionists who do believe literally in Noah's Flood that such a Flood negates uniformitarian geology which, in turn, negates the billions of years during which evolution is supposed to have happened, he does not know what else he can say.

At this point the writer turns to Catholics who believe what the Church teaches but do not believe literally in the world-wide flood described in *Genesis*. Catholics may not have heard that there was a Pope who, for our belief, taught about Noah's flood according to *Genesis*. He predicted that "scoffers" will "deliberately ignore this fact that by the word of God heavens existed long ago, and an earth formed out of water and by means of water, through which the world that then existed was deluged with water and perished." Not only that, this Pope taught that when that ancient world perished because God brought a flood upon it, He waited patiently while Noah built the ark in which eight persons were saved. That Pope was Peter. Read it in 1 Peter 3:20, 2 Peter 2:5 and 2 Peter 3:5-6. Catholics are taught that Scripture is true. Why is it that Evangelicals put more belief in our Pope's teaching about the *Genesis* flood than many Catholic scholars and priests do? See also *Hebrews* 11:7 where Paul writes that God warned Noah and Noah constructed an ark for saving his household.

If one doubts the first Pope and the Apostle to the Gentiles, will one believe it from the lips of the Second Person of the Trinity? Read it in Matthew 24:28.

> For as in those days before the flood they were eating and drinking, marrying and giving in marriage, until the day when Noah entered the ark, and they did not know until the flood came and swept them all away, so will be the coming of the Son of man.

Some might think that Jesus must have been talking about a local flood. Do they also think that Our Lord made a stupid comparison by equating the impact of a local flood with the world-wide impact of His Second Coming?

You and the Wives of Noah's Three Sons

One type of DNA is passed from generation to generation only through mothers. This genetic material is known as mitochondrial DNA or mtDNA. Typically, a sperm carries mitochondria in its tail as an energy source for its long journey to the egg. When the sperm attaches to the egg during fertilization, the tail falls off. Consequently, the only mitochondria the new human gets are from the egg its mother provided. Ancestry testing has become popular based on new knowledge of genetics. There are three types of genealogical DNA tests. One of those, mtDNA, tests a man or woman along his/her direct maternal line. Research biologist Dr. Nathanial Jeanson plotted hundreds of human mtDNA sequences and the project revealed an obvious pattern: The mtDNA stemmed from three central "trunks" or nodes instead of just the one commonly known as mitochondrial Eve. Jeanson's data suggests that the wives of Noah's three sons best explain that finding. http://www.icr.org/article/new-dna-study-confirms-noah/

Genesis and Marriage

Some Catholics mock Evangelicals with the term "Fundamentalists" for taking the Creation and Flood accounts in *Genesis* literally. Yet many of those same Catholics take Jesus' teaching on marriage literally. (And sadly, many don't.) According to Mark 10:6-8, Jesus said: "But from the beginning of creation 'God made them male and female.' 'For this reason a man shall leave his father and mother and be joined to his wife, and the two shall become one.' So they are no longer two but one." Jesus was quoting from chapters 1 and 2 of *Genesis*. These are the same chapters that theistic evolutionists say can't be taken literally. Why would Jesus quote literally from those chapters to give His definitive teaching on marriage if He didn't intend for us to believe them literally? And notice that He said that they were male and female from the beginning of creation, not after millions of years of evolution. The parallel passage to Mark 10 on marriage, Matthew 19: 4-5, reads:

> Have you not read that **he who created them** from the beginning made them male and female, and **said,** 'Therefore a man shall leave his father and his mother and hold fast to his wife, and the two shall become one flesh'?

Genesis 1-2 from which Jesus quoted is just part of the author's narrative, yet Jesus stated that it was said by the One who made Adam and Eve. Jesus affirmed that what Genesis says, God said!

The Catechism of the Catholic Church, in its teaching about marriage in paragraphs 1604-1607, quotes from *Genesis* 1 and 2 seven times. Leo XIII made the connection between *Genesis* and marriage in his encyclical *Arcanum divinae*.

> The true origin of marriage, venerable brothers, is well known to all . . .We record what is to all known, and cannot be doubted by any, that God, on the sixth day of creation, having made man from the slime of the earth, and having breathed into his face the breath of life, gave him a companion, whom He miraculously took from the side of Adam when he was locked in sleep . . . And this union of man and woman . . . even from the beginning manifested chiefly two most excellent properties . . . namely, unity and perpetuity

The Catechism, #2169 on our Sunday obligation, quotes Scripture: "For in six days the Lord made heaven and earth, the sea, and all that is in them, and rested on the seventh day; therefore the Lord blessed the Sabbath day and hollowed it." Catholic evolutionists accept the Sunday obligation but believe in "creation" over billions of years. Go figure.

What God Is This?

Is it consistent with the character of God to reveal an account of His *fiat* creation and then to allow all Fathers, Doctors and Popes to believe and proclaim that account, as written, for almost two thousand years, only to "enlighten" the Church with an evolutionary account of origins through the speculations of men like Hutton, Lyell, Darwin, and Gould? And, if it is, who in his right mind would trust such an incompetent, self-contradictory "god"?

Chapter 6-Evolution is Secular Theology

Charles Darwin is most recognized for postulating the theory of evolution through his book *Origin of Species...* that was first published in 1859. However, it was his German colleague Ernst Haeckel who may have been responsible for causing the theory to infiltrate Catholicism primarily through the Jesuits.

Haeckel (1834–1919) was a professor of zoology and marine biologist, as well as a qualified medical doctor who was involved at the University of Jena during most of his academic lifetime. Haeckel produced a set of drawings known historically as "Haeckel's embryos" that purported to show that humans in the womb went through the stages from which we allegedly evolved. In his 1868 book *Natürliche Schöpfungsgeschichte* (The History of Natural Creation) Ernst Haeckel suggested that he had made various comparisons using human, monkey and dog embryos. The drawings he produced consisted of nearly identical embryos. Based on these drawings, Haeckel then suggested that the life forms involved had common origins.

In a *Science* article published in 1997, "Haeckel's Embryos: Fraud Rediscovered," Haeckel, was indicted of having intentionally misrepresented embryological development. The article reported that the work of evolutionist Michael Richardson and his colleagues demonstrated this malfeasance through a comparison of Haeckel's illustrations of early-stage embryos with photographs of the same species at a comparable stage The photos showed embryos of various species that differed among themselves and certainly from Haeckel's images. The differences were striking and the implication obvious: fraudulent misrepresentation. Richardson, as quoted in the article, affirmed the charge: "It looks like it's turning out to be one of the most famous fakes in biology."

An exceptionally good and well-researched article (by a Muslim) that explains the fraud in detail and its enormous influence on biology and physiology education that should be read is here:

https://www.harunyahya.com/en/Articles/19164/haeckels-embryo-drawings-are-fraudulent

Haeckel and the Catholic Church

Haeckel's bogus "proof" was the single most effective piece of propaganda in the campaign to convince the intellectual elite of the Western world that microbe-to-man evolution was a scientific fact rather than a wild conjecture. Hugh Owen, Director of the Kolbe Center for the Study of Creation, has explained how the fraud began its spread into mainstream Catholic education

> It convinced Catholic intellectuals from [American] Fr. John Augustine Zahm at Notre Dame at the dawn of the twentieth century to [German] Fr. Karl Rahner towards the end of the twentieth century that the traditional teaching of the Church on the special creation of Adam and Eve had been falsified by this "scientific" discovery. Haeckel himself acknowledged how quickly the intellectual elite of the Catholic Church changed its position on evolution.

Fr. Zahm (1851-1921) was a professor of physics at ND. His 1896 book, *Evolution and Dogma*, was very influential. In this text, as in his others, Zahm argued that Roman Catholicism could fully accept an evolutionary view of biological systems, as long as this view was not centered around Darwin's theory of natural selection. After the Vatican censured the book in 1898, Zahm fully accepted this rebuttal and pulled away from any writing concerning the relationship of theology and science. His obedience notwithstanding, Fr. Zahm's book and theology remained a fixture in Notre Dame's teaching by a faculty that accepted Darwinism as a proved fact. It was used throughout the Catholic higher education system. I found it in the library of a self-described "orthodox" college that has a large collection of books promoting both atheistic and theistic evolution. The book is still available from online book sellers.

Fr. Karl Rahner (1904-1984), a Jesuit, was one of the most influential theologians of the 20th century. His 6-volume *Theological Investigations* was a staple in seminaries around the world and did enormous harm. It may have been his belief in Haeckel's embryos that made him a dissenter to *Humanae Vitae*.

In his 1906 book, *Last Words on Evolution,* Haeckel observed

...the interesting efforts that the Church has lately made to enter into a peaceful compromise with its deadly enemy, Monistic science. It has decided to accept to a certain extent, and to accommodate to its creed (in a distorted and mutilated form) the doctrine of evolution, which it has vehemently opposed for thirty years. This remarkable change of front on the part of the Church militant seemed to me so interesting and important, and at the same time so misleading and mischievous ... Our science of evolution won its greatest triumph when, at the beginning of the twentieth century, its most powerful opponents, the Churches, became reconciled to it, and endeavored to bring their dogmas into line with it.

Haeckel could not have been referring to the Magisterium when he referred to "the Church" because it wasn't the Pope or Vatican Congregations who accepted evolution. It was the clerical intellectuals. Hugh Owen added that Haeckel went on to note the unique role played by scientists within the Society of Jesus in accomplishing this revolution against the "foundations" of the Creed. Haeckel wrote:

> The Jesuit Father Wasmann, and his colleagues, have - unwittingly - done a very great service to the progress of pure science. The Catholic Church, the most powerful and widespread of the Christian sects, sees itself compelled to capitulate to the idea of evolution. It embraces the most important application of the idea, Lamarck and Darwin's theory of descent, which it had vigorously combated until twenty years ago. It does, indeed, mutilate the great tree, cutting off its roots and its highest branch; it rejects spontaneous generation or archigony at the bottom, and the descent of man from animal ancestors above. But these exceptions will not last. Impartial biology will take no notice of them, and the religious creed will at length determine that the more complex species have been evolved from a series of simpler forms according to Darwinian principles . . .The open acknowledgment of the truth of evolution by the Jesuit, Father Wasmann, deserves careful attention, and we may look forward to a further development. If his force of conviction and his moral courage are strong enough, he will go on to draw the normal conclusions from his high scientific attainments and leave the Catholic Church, as the prominent Jesuits, Count Hoensbroech and the able geologist, Professor Renard of Ghent, one of the workers on the deep-sea deposits in the *Challenger* expedition, have lately done. But even if this does not happen, his recognition of Darwinism, in the name of Christian belief, will remain a landmark in the history of evolution. His ingenious and very Jesuitical attempt to bring together the opposite poles will have no very mischievous effect; it will rather tend to hasten the victory

of the scientific conception of evolution over the mystic beliefs of the Churches.

Hugh Owen pointed out that

> With this statement Haeckel showed keen insight into the weakness of theistic evolutionist attempts to reconcile molecules-to-man evolution with the antithetical dogma of creation. He rightly anticipated that if Catholic theologians accepted the naturalistic accounts of Darwin and his disciples for the origin of man and other living things and abandoned the constant teaching of the Church on the fundamental doctrine of creation, thoughtful Catholics would realize the absurdity of trying to reconcile these opposites. He realized that theologians who allowed natural scientists to dictate to them in regard to the dogma of creation would end up ceding the primacy of theology as the Queen of the Sciences and allow Natural Science to usurp her place. Haeckel also noted the irony that Jesuits and other Catholic apologists for theistic evolution at the end of the nineteenth century tried to make it seem as if the Church had "admitted the theory of evolution for decades" when just a decade or two before the Church had been united against evolution as a mortal threat to the very foundations of the Faith.

Haeckel, in continuing his verbal "victory lap," commented on another Jesuit of note:

> We find a similar diplomatic retreat in the popular work of the Jesuit, Father Martin Gander, *The Theory of Descent* (1904): "Thus the modern forms of matter were not immediately created by God; they are effects of the formative forces, which were put by the creator in the primitive matter, and gradually came into view in the course of the earth's history, when the external conditions

were given in the proper combination." That is a remarkable change of front on the part of the clergy.

George Tyrrell (1861-1909) and Alfred Loisy (1857-1940), were among other Jesuits who, because of their acceptance of evolution, specialized in the rejection of any idea of supernatural revelation. It is most probable that "evolution is a proved fact" was taught in all of those once great Jesuit universities which, like those in the U.S., (Georgetown, Marquette, Boston College) have become leaders in heterodox Catholicism. The aforementioned university and seminary biblical professor and Vincentian priest Bruce Vawter published in 1956 a popular book, *A Path Through Genesis*. It had an enormous impact in the theological community leading many to the common belief that evolution happened but "God did it" and the Divine Revelation of Genesis was what? According to Bishop Barron, chairman of the U.S. Bishops' Committee for Catechetics and Evangelization, it is not the historical narrative it seems; it is "theology, mysticism, spirituality; a theological reflection on the origin of all things." As exemplified by James Fitzpatrick's testimony about what he was taught by Marist brothers and Jesuits, it is a fact that sisters, brothers, and priests in the 1950's were teaching high-school students to believe in evolution.

Evolution Ushers in "Theology Fiction"
Jesuit belief in evolution was established in the 19th century but accelerated early in the 20th Century, in part, because of the scientific reputation and evolutionary theological writings of another one of their own, Frenchman Pierre Teilhard de Chardin, S.J. Pierre Teilhard de Chardin's greatest contribution to the theological waywardness of the Jesuits was through his writings. Fr. Victor Warkulwiz, M.S.S., credited de Chardin with introducing a new genre of literature, namely, theology fiction. It was mystical evolutionary poetry and prose that, according to Fr.

Warkulwiz, mesmerized many Catholics with a "seductive merging of the spiritual and the secular." According to Fr. Warkulwiz, "His writings create havoc with Catholic notions about creation, redemption, sanctification, original and actual sin, evil and grace." In 1957, this theology fiction caused the Vatican's Congregation for the Doctrine of the Faith, then called "the Holy Office," to order that his works be removed from libraries of Catholic institutions and forbade their sale in Catholic bookstores. In 1962, about when Mr. Fitzpatrick was being taught by Jesuits at Fordham, there came another document warning the faithful about errors and ambiguities in de Chardin's writings. Obviously, those warnings were, and continue to be, ignored. This writer's wife recalled seeing de Chardin's *The Phenomenon of Man* and *The Divine Milieu* being passed around among the students at her Catholic women's college circa 1962. His books were published and republished. At least nine of his books are for sale online.

The Greatest Discovery

Fr. de Chardin's influence on the Jesuits' theological and philosophical traditions came, in part, from his reputation as a paleontologist. Fr. de Chardin's reputation was greatly enhanced because of his significant role in what was heralded as the greatest paleontological discovery of all time, namely, the Piltdown Man. Piltdown Man is the name given to some fragments of a jawbone and a skull unearthed in close proximity to each other in an English gravel pit by paleontologist Charles Dawson in 1912. Although questioned by some, they were widely regarded to be fossilized bones of an ape partially evolved into a man. In 1913, while digging with Dawson, de Chardin discovered a canine tooth that seemed to provide the confirming evidence. From 1913, these fragments became recognized by the scientific consensus as the "missing link" in the descent of man from a lower animal. It was the proof through fossil evidence that Darwin predicted would be discovered when he published his theory of biological evolution in 1859. Piltdown Man, with plaster filling in the missing parts of the fossil according to the imagination of Dawson the paleontologist credited with the discovery, was prominently exhibited in the British Museum as an example of human evolution until it was discovered to be a complete forgery. The jawbone was that of an orangutan that had been doctored. It was proved to be a forgery in 1953. That was after generations of school children worldwide including the above-mentioned Mr. Fitzpatrick and recent Popes when as schoolboys had studied textbooks with artist conception drawings of "Eoanthropus dawsoni," a half man-half ape complete with hunched back, hairy body and a "knowing" look in his eye. They had been told that the Piltdown Man was their ancestor. And most believed it. Gary Parker, Ed. D., in an article in *Acts & Facts*, observed in 1981:

> At least Piltdown answers one often-asked question: "Can virtually all scientists be wrong about such an important matter as human origins?" The answer, most emphatically, is: "Yes, and it wouldn't be the first time." Over 500 doctoral dissertations were done on Piltdown Man, yet all this intense scientific scrutiny failed to expose the fake.

Evolutionary Belief in the 1920s

Thanks to Piltdown Man and America's most influential philosopher, John Dewey, belief in evolution became the mainstream belief in U.S. secular universities in the beginning of the 20th century even if it took a few decades to become mainstream in the public schools. A practical demonstration of that was the so-called "Scopes Monkey Trial" that took place in Tennessee in 1925. A high-school teacher, John Scopes, collaborated to create a case for the American Civil Liberties Union (ACLU) to contest Tennessee law. Scopes volunteered to

be tried for violating the law which only prohibited the teaching that humans evolved from animals. Scopes used *Civic Biology,* a 1914 book that promoted human evolution from animals, racism, and eugenics. Read about that book here to understand how it promoted racism in America.
https://evolutionnews.org/2007/07/an_uncivic_biology/.

In the trial, Scopes was defended by a famous defense lawyer and ACLU member named Clarence Darrow who introduced the Piltdown Man as part of the scientific defense. A very interesting summary of the Scopes Trial and the lasting influence on American education is here: https://creation.com/scopes-at-100

Vestigial Structures

In addition to Piltdown Man, the Scopes Trial also showcased another belief of the 1925 scientific consensus, namely, vestigial structures. The term (in evolution speak) means genetically determined structures or attributes that have apparently lost most or all of their ancestral function in a given species, but have been retained through evolution. This is 19th Century Darwin theory that can be summarized as "use it or lose it." According to Darwin, the effect of "use" strengthens and enlarges certain body parts. But Darwin claimed that the species have been modified by the inherited effects of the use and disuse of parts. Science in Darwin's era preceded the science of genetics.

Darwin wasn't the first believer in evolution. It was a hot topic among Naturalists since the Greek philosophers and it was "in the air" of the 18th Century. Because the rudimentary science of that era did not know what certain body parts were for, they assumed they were left over from a lower form from which humans were thought to have evolved. In 1798 a Frenchman noted that

> Whereas useless in this circumstance, these rudiments...
> have not been eliminated, because Nature never works by

rapid jumps, and She always leaves vestiges of an organ, even though it is completely superfluous, if that organ plays an important role in the other species of the same family.

The term "vestigial" was coined later by a 19th Century scientist influenced by Darwin's "use it or lose it" theory. A German, Robert Wiedersheim, in 1893 published a list of 86 human organs that he said had "lost their original physiological significance" and he attributed that to evolution. The 19th Century evolutionists didn't know what God's purpose was for currently observable things in humans so they considered them as leftovers from a previous stage of evolution. By 1925, Wiedersheim's list had grown from 86 to 180. Wiedersheim's list was introduced at the Scopes Trial with the comment that a human had so many vestigial structures left over from evolution that he was a veritable walking museum of antiquities.

19th Century Science on Wikipedia

It's almost funny to read the evolutionists commentary on structures when they make up excuses to still regard human body parts as vestigial. Look up the Wikipedia entry for the word "Vestigiality." The appendix was a favorite example of a useless, vestigial structure by "experts" from Darwin to Harvard's Ernst Mayr; but then it was discovered to be an important factor in regulating the level of gut microflora and includes major functions such as metabolic activities that result in the salvage of energy and absorbable nutrients, on immune structure and function, and protection against foreign microbes. In the following, notice how the evolutionist Wikipedia writer first presents an evolutionary assumption as a fact before admitting that the appendix is useful.

A classic example at the level of gross anatomy is the human vermiform appendix — though vestigial in the

111

sense of retaining no significant *digestive* function, the appendix still has immunological roles and is useful in maintaining gut flora.

What evidence is there that the appendix *ever* had a digestive function except the assumption that it did? Here is another example

> The coccyx or tailbone, though a vestige of the tail of some primate ancestors, is functional as an anchor for certain pelvic muscles including: the levator ani muscle and the largest gluteal muscle, the gluteus maximus.

That humans had an ancestor is a big enough fairy tale without adding that the ancestor had a tail.

> The emergence of vestigiality occurs by normal evolutionary processes, typically by loss of function of a feature that is no longer subject to positive selection pressures when it loses its value in a changing environment. More urgently the feature may be selected against when its function becomes definitely harmful. Typical examples of both types occur in the loss of flying capability in island-dwelling species.

In other words, evolution, "knowing" that the island birds had no need to leave the island, decided to devolve the flying ability it took billions of years for them to evolve from when they were fish or whatever because they might fly out over the ocean and forget how to get home. That function would be "definitely harmful." Or, maybe because the birds knew they had nowhere to go, they started walking around the island and failing to heed Mr. Darwin's dictum to "use it or lose it," they lost their flying ability.

112

More nonsense from Wikipedia:

> Humans also bear some vestigial behaviors and reflexes. The formation of goose bumps in humans under stress is a vestigial reflex. Its function in human ancestors was to raise the body's hair, making the ancestor appear larger and scaring off predators.

Catholic children in schools have been taught nonsense like this for a long time. Catholic theistic evolutionists were made, not born.

Whale Sex: It Is in the Hips

For years, evolutionists have pointed to certain small bones in whales as vestiges. According to evolutionary theory, the whales' ancestor had legs. When that ancestor went to sea, through non use, the legs were lost and those bones are all that is left. A September 8, 2014, release from the University of Southern California disproved that theory. The university published a story on its website titled, "Whale Sex: it's all in the hips." In the article, it announced

> New research turns a long-accepted evolutionary assumption on its head – finding that far from being just vestigial, whale pelvic bones play a key role in reproduction.

And now that they are shown to be necessary, what evidence is there that they are vestigial of anything? That whales could ever have evolved from land animals is tooth-fairy science. For a great description of the amazing unique design of whales and the flimsy "science" behind the myth of their evolution from a land animal see *Zombie Science* (Discovery Institute, 2017) chapter 5. For more discussion about vestigial propaganda see http://creation.com/do-any-vestigial-organs-exist-in-humans

All of the "Links" are Missing

Darwin theorized that individuals acquired beneficial characteristics and passed them on by natural selection or "survival of the fittest." In this view, evolution is seen as generally smooth and continuous. It required that there be some evidence of "in between" things which are called transitional fossils. That explains the scientific excitement generated by Piltdown Man, the hoped for "link" between humans and their supposed non-human ancestors. The fossils known in Darwin's time showed fully-formed individuals although some were subjects of further debate. Some were thought to be of something that had become extinct and some were the same as living things of his era. Darwin explained that transitional fossils hadn't been found because relatively few fossils had been found. According to Darwin, the reason so few had been found was because the earth's crust had been formed by natural processes such as volcanoes, ice movement, wind, rain and erosion. That was the 18th Century uniformitarian theory of geology which, if true, projected the age of the earth to be billions of years. Under those natural conditions, nature would work against a dead organism becoming fossilized. For example, dead animals would be eaten by other animals or birds and their bones would be scattered. If they got buried before they had been picked over, the effects of wind, rain, floods, etc. could uncover them.

When archeology became a much more systematic discipline in the late 19th century and became a widely used tool for historical and anthropological research in the 20th century, more fossils than Darwin ever imagined were unearthed. Millions of fossils have been found. The world's museums are full of fossils. For example, between 1909 and 1915 the Smithsonian Museum collected over 65,000 specimens, many very well preserved, from a site in British Columbia known as the Burgess Shale. These mostly sea creatures are found at 7,500 feet up in the Canadian

Rockies. These complex animals had apparently "risen" suddenly, distinct, and fully formed, with nothing by way of ancestor forms. Other massive deposits of fossils, distinct and fully formed from the same so-called Cambrian geologic age were discovered in the mid-1980s in southern China. The "Chengjiang Fossils" are an even greater variety, including soft-body animals, than the Burgess Shale.

Hopeful Monster

Richard B. Goldschmidt (d.1958) was a famous geneticist. He is considered the first to integrate genetics, development, and evolution. He did important work that advanced the science of genetics. He wrote that at age sixteen

> ...it seemed that all problems of heaven and earth were solved simply and convincingly; there was an answer to every question which troubled the young mind. Evolution was the key to everything and could replace all the beliefs and creeds which one was discarding. There was no creation, no God, no heaven and hell, only evolution and the wonderful law of recapitulation [in the womb] which demonstrated the fact of evolution to the most stubborn believer in creation.

The "law of recapitulation" that teenager Goldschmidt believed is an example of how influential Ernst Haeckel's embryos were. In *Natural History*, March 2000, Harvard's atheist science professor Stephen Jay Gould wrote that we should be "astonished and ashamed by the century of mindless recycling that has led to the persistence of these drawings in a large number, if not the majority, of modern textbooks." Nevertheless, this fraudulent "science" continues to be perpetuated in textbooks including two titled *Biology* by different authors published in 2014. Many other examples of recently-published biology textbooks with these fake drawings are given in *Zombie Science*. In a "debate" via

Facebook my anti-evolutionism was ridiculed by a Catholic obstetrician who said I "obviously had never studied embryology." She probably studied Haeckel's embryos in college and may have used the popular textbook by Douglas Futuyma, *Evolutionary Biology*, in which he wrote that "early in development human embryos are almost indistinguishable from those of fishes." Following a debate with a representative of Planned Parenthood at a public high school in which my wife showed slides of human fetal development, a girl came up to her in tears and said "I had an abortion. They told me at my stage it was a fish."

When Goldschmidt grew up and became a scientist, he was uncomfortable with the lack of transitional fossils. He postulated a theory to explain the sudden appearance in the fossil record of fully-formed specimens. Goldschmidt advanced a model of macroevolution [big changes] through macromutations [big mutations] that is popularly known as the "Hopeful Monster" hypothesis. In this context, Goldschmidt meant the big jumps that were made by evolution from one fully-formed species to the next "more complex" fully-formed species without intermediate forms were because of really, really big mutations.

Punctuated Equilibrium

Perhaps the term "Hopeful Monster" was a bit of an embarrassment to evolutionists until that consummate story-spinner and Harvard professor Stephen Jay Gould solved the problem. He refined and changed the name of the theory. With Harvard colleague Niles Eldredge, Gould proposed "punctuated equilibrium." Eldredge and Gould proposed that the degree of gradualism commonly attributed to Darwin's theory is virtually nonexistent in the fossil record, and that stasis (no change) dominates the history of most fossil species. In plain speak, there are no more than a handful of possible transitional fossils about which even evolutionists dispute. Essentially, the intermediate "links" are not missing, they were never existent.

Punctuated equilibrium is a refinement to evolutionary theory. It describes patterns of descent taking place in "fits and starts" separated by long periods of stability. Punctuated Equilibrium sounds better than Hopeful Monster but it's essentially the same theory. One only has to examine Punctuated Equilibrium to see a typical example of evolutionist fog. This is how Gould and Eldredge explained it in 1977 in *Paleobiology*:

> Punctuated equilibrium proposes that most species will exhibit little net evolutionary change for most of their geological history, remaining in an extended state called *stasis*. When significant evolutionary change occurs, the theory proposes that it is generally restricted to rare and rapid (on a geologic time scale)) events of branching speciation called cladogenesis.

Sounds impressive, right? What is cladogenesis? According to the authors, cladogenesis is the process by which a species splits into two distinct species, rather than one species gradually transforming into another. Get it? The species dog splits into cats and chickens. Why do Harvard professors write such nutty stuff? They know that all of the entirely different species did not "evolve" gradually as Darwin proposed because there are no transitions. Yet they "know" that the various distinct species are the result of evolution. So, if species didn't change into different species slowly through small changes, they must have changed into different species rapidly through big changes they had been storing up for a long, long time. Because it is a theory, it qualifies as "science."

Around in a Circle

In 1980, also in the journal *Paleobiology*, Gould said punctuated equilibrium was a "new and general theory" of evolution and that neo-Darwinism is "effectively dead, despite its persistence as textbook orthodoxy." According to Dr. Stephen Meyer in *Darwin's Doubt* it was "only after critics exposed punctuated equilibrium for lacking an adequate mechanism did Gould retreat to a more conservative formulation of the theory, making its reliance upon the neo-Darwinian mechanism explicit." In other words, according to Meyer,

> advocates of punctuated equilibrium were forced to concede both the inadequacy of their proposed mechanisms and to rely on the neo-Darwinian process of mutation and natural selection in order to account for the origin of new genetic traits and anatomical innovations…Thus, though the theory of punctuated equilibrium was initially presented as a solution to the mysterious and sudden origin of animal forms, upon closer inspection, it failed to offer such a solution.

No Evolution Proves Evolution

In the Gould-Eldredge punctuated equilibrium fig leaf, "most species will exhibit little net evolutionary change for most of their geological history, remaining in an extended state called *stasis*." Stasis means a period or state of inactivity or equilibrium. Evolutionists even claim that by remaining in an indefinite period of inactivity, that is, by staying exactly the same, evolutionary theory is demonstrated. "By not evolving, deep sea microbes may prove Darwin right" is the news report of a 2015 paper published in *Proceedings of the National Academy of Science*. The paper is about three communities of bacteria, two of which were found fossilized and one is living off the west coast of South America. The first fossils are in a rock which according to evolution-based dating methods is 2.3 billion years old. The second fossils are in a rock evolutionary dating indicates is 1.8 billion years old. All of the samples are identical.

According to J. William Schopf, a paleobiologist at UCLA: "In form, function and metabolism, they are identical,"

> Researchers say these microscopic organisms are an example of "extreme evolutionary stasis" and represent the greatest lack of evolution ever seen. They may also, paradoxically, prove that Darwin's theory of evolution is true.

Scientists from the Institute for Creation Research pointed out the obvious: "evolutionary stasis is an oxymoron." When a complete lack of difference is counted as evidence for evolution, and all other differences are attributed to evolution, it shows that evolution is an arbitrary and unfalsifiable assumption—not even a hypothesis.

While on the subject of wacky evolutionists, consider this March 2015 online report of an article published in *Genome Biology:* "Evolutionary tree: Humans may have evolved with plant genes, study claims"

> Humans may have evolved with the genes of plants, fungi and micro-organisms, according to a consensus-challenging Cambridge University study. The study into the literal roots of mankind builds on, and to some extent confirms, the findings of a 2001 investigation into whether or not humans could have acquired DNA from plants... "We may need to re-evaluate how we think about evolution."

Evolutionists Discovered Genetics?

In the 1860s Augustinian monk Gregor Mendel performed experiments that, when recognized and validated nearly 40 years later, provided the basis for the new science of genetics. Darwinian evolution, though still taught to school children, was replaced by a new theory called Neo-Darwinism. Evolutionists define Neo-Darwinism as the "modern synthesis" of Darwinian evolution through natural selection with Mendelian genetics. Neo-Darwinism is the view that evolution is due to the natural selection of variations that originate as gene mutations. (As will be explained below, gene mutations are harmful, not beneficial.) Evolutionists kept Darwin's name alive perhaps to shield the fact that observational genetics of the here and now gave Darwinism a kick in the teeth. In their desperate attempt to "rescue" Darwin some evolutionists have made the absurd claim that Darwinism led to the discovery of genetics. For example, in May 2015 in a blog defending the reliability of a "scientific consensus," theoretical astrophysicist Ethan Siegel wrote:

> Think about evolution, for example. Many people still rally against it, claiming that it's impossible. Yet evolution was the consensus position that led to the discovery of genetics, and genetics itself was the consensus that allowed us to discover DNA, the "code" behind genetics, inherited traits and evolution.

In response to Ethan Siegel, EvolutionNews.org published an excerpt from the *Politically Incorrect Guide to Darwinism and Intelligent Design* that pointed out that Mendel found Darwin "unpersuasive." Darwin believed cells contained what he called "gemmules" that transmit characteristics in a "blending process" Darwin called "pangenesis." According to Darwin these "gemmules" change by use or disuse. That's the basis for his "use it or lose it" that evolutionists still believe in when they refer to flightless birds or whales that supposedly began as land animals and lost their legs.

> Mendel's theory of stable factors contradicted Darwin's theory of changeable gemmules. Thus, although Mendel's work was published in 1866, Darwinists totally ignored it for more than three decades. William Bateson, one of the scientists who "rediscovered" Mendelian genetics at the

turn of the century, wrote that the cause for this lack of interest was "unquestionably to be found in that neglect of the experimental study of the problem of Species which supervened on the general acceptance of the Darwinian doctrines."

In other words, the scientific consensus was so enamored by Darwinism that they saw no need for alternative theories until there was so much evidence that Mendel was right.

Is Evolution of Any Scientific Value at All?

Which raises the question: Does evolution have any scientific value at all? Evolutionist Dr. Marc Kirschner, founding chair of the Department of Systems Biology at Harvard Medical School was quoted in the October 23, 2005 *Boston Globe* as having stated:

> In fact, over the last 100 years, almost all of biology has preceded independent of evolution, except evolutionary biology itself. Molecular biology, biochemistry, physiology, have not taken evolution into account at all.

In similar vein, the anti-creationist Larry Witham wrote:

> Surprisingly, however, the most notable aspect of natural scientists in assembly is how little they focus on evolution. Its day-to-day irrelevance is a great 'paradox' in biology, according to a *BioEssays* special issue on evolution in 2000. 'While the great majority of biologists would probably agree with Theodosius Dobzhansky's dictum that "Nothing in biology makes sense except in the light of evolution," most can conduct their work quite happily without particular reference to evolutionary ideas', the editor wrote. 'Evolution would appear to be the indispensable unifying idea and, at the same time, a highly superfluous one.' (Witham, Larry A., *Where*

121

Darwin Meets the Bible: Creationists and Evolutionists in America (hardcover), p. 43, Oxford University Press, 2002)

Evolution contributes nothing tangible to science but that doesn't mean that hoary 19th Century notions can't be used to sell books to the gullible public. Cardiologist Lee Goldman, dean of the College of Physicians and Surgeons, chief executive of Columbia University Medical Center in a 2015 diet book aimed at the general public titled *Too Much of a Good Thing,* wrote:

> Can't stick to a diet? That's a holdover from when humans roamed the plains and gorged when food was plentiful, storing the rest as fat for when it wasn't. Anxiety is a descendant of the fight-or-flight response, which kept us alive when faced with a woolly mammoth but is something that we less often need today.

Is that medical science or something he learned in high school? Medical doctors find evolution theory useless because they are more like results-oriented engineers than theoretical scientists inhabiting academia. Evolution is a "white elephant"-big and useless. Michael Egnor of the Discovery Institute observed that

> Darwinists use "evolution" because it's their creation myth and because its regular invocation is required by their thought police. Doctors and medical researchers don't use "evolution" because it's irrelevant to medical research. Fairy tales about survival of survivors contribute nothing to medical research, or to any other research. The extraordinary success of medical research is glaring confirmation of antibiotic pioneer Philip Skell's observation that reference to evolution in biology is just a "narrative gloss" on the real science. Just-so stories contribute nothing to biology. Medical research is wildly successful, without any significant reference to evolution.

At http://www.dissentfromdarwin.org read the list of 950 Ph. D. scientists who have signed their name to the following statement:

> We are skeptical of claims for the ability of random mutations and natural selection to account for the complexity of life. Careful examination of the evidence for Darwinian theory should be encouraged.

"Darwin of the 20th Century" Frustrated by Genetics

Ernst Mayr, an atheist, published *What Evolution Is*. Dr. Mayr was hailed by the *NY Times* as "the Darwin of the 20th Century." At the time of the book's publication in 2001, Dr. Mayr had published 14 books on evolutionary biology and zoology and was Professor Emeritus in the Museum of Comparative Zoology at Harvard University. In the Preface to his book, Dr. Mayr complained that

> …most treatments of evolution are written in a reductionist manner in which all evolutionary phenomena are reduced to the level of the gene. An attempt is then made to explain the higher-level evolutionary process by "upward" reasoning. This approach invariably fails.

What Dr. Mayr meant by "upward reasoning" is the effort to explain macroevolution based on reasoning "upward" from microevolution. To see why that approach "invariably fails" one must understand what each of those two terms mean. A good explanation by Dr. John D. Morris follows.

> *Micro*evolution refers to varieties within a given type. Change happens within a group, but the descendant is clearly of the same type as the ancestor. This might better be called variation, or adaptation, but the changes are "horizontal" in effect, not "vertical."

All creation-supporting scientists agree that microevolution as described above, "horizontal," is non-controversial. The disagreement concerns the alleged "vertical" evolution. Darwin's second major work was *The Descent of Man* and the notion that all the species descended from one ancestor is the modern synthesis of evolution. Thus, the term "vertical" is used to mean the flow of evolution in a vertical direction. Picture a family tree with your two sets of great grandparents at the top and you at the bottom. Your position on the chart as a descendent of your great grandparents would be vertically below them with your other ancestors above you. In your family tree, all of your ancestors would be humans. In an evolutionary family tree, your pre-historic ancestors would be a variety of different and unique animals. (They would be different and unique because of "punctuated equilibrium," remember.) You may not look at all like your great grandparents, but this is because there are other fully-human genes brought into the family's gene pool by the spouses of your great grandparents' descendants, who were not descendants of those great grandparents. The only genes they could bring into the gene pool were their human genes.

Microevolution by Artificial Selection

A fairly recent new breed is a Labradoodle. It is a crossbreed of the Labrador Retriever and the Standard, Miniature, or Toy Poodle. The term first appeared in 1955, but was not popularized until 1988, when the mix began to be used as an allergen-free guide dog. Both crossbred animals were of the same species. It is sometimes possible to crossbreed animals from different species but when that is done the offspring are sterile. For example, a mule is the sterile offspring of crossbreeding a horse with a donkey. According to Dr. Morris

> The small or *micro*evolutionary changes occur by recombining existing genetic material within the group. As Gregor Mendel observed with his breeding studies on peas in the mid 1800's, there are natural limits to genetic change. A population of organisms can vary only so much.

124

Evolutionists take those known types of micro changes, postulate beneficial mutations that have never been observed, theorize "punctuated equilibrium" resulting from stored up mutations, mix in a few billion years, and triumphantly declare for our belief that it scientifically explains macroevolution, the supposed origin of all of the unique types of living things. Dr. Morris explains:

> *Macro*evolution refers to major evolutionary changes over time, the origin of new types of organisms from previously existing, but different, ancestral types. Examples of this would be fish descending from an invertebrate animal, or whales descending from a land mammal. The evolutionary concept demands these bizarre changes. Evolutionists assume that the small, horizontal *micro*evolutionary changes (which are observed) lead to large, vertical macroevolutionary changes (which are never observed). This philosophical leap of faith lies at the eve of evolution thinking.

Mutations Remove Genetic Information

Genetic mutations do occur because of what might be thought of as "copying errors" in the DNA code. These are not beneficial because they don't add information, they remove information. Once they occur, they can be passed along through reproduction. A genetic disorder is a condition caused by an absent or defective gene or by a chromosomal aberration. Medical research has identified specific human gene flaws as markers for certain diseases or conditions. On the other hand, beneficial mutations have not been observed. One that has often been cited in evolution propaganda is sickle-cell anemia that provides an individual with enhanced resistance to malaria. However, sickle-cell anemia is a serious and sometimes fatal blood disorder. See http://creation.com/exposing-evolutions-icon. Dr. Morris explained how textbooks use examples of microevolution to "sell" belief in macroevolution to children:

A review of any biology textbook will include a discussion of *micro*evolutionary changes. This list will include the variety of beak shape among the finches of the Galapagos Islands. Always mentioned is the peppered moth in England, a population of moths whose dominant color in the population shifted during the Industrial Revolution, when soot covered the trees. [And recent research indicates the data was faked.] While in each case, observed change was limited to *micro*evolution, the inference is that these minor changes can be extrapolated over many generations to *macro*evolution.

In that paragraph Dr. Morris mentioned the style of evolutionary writing that this writer pointed out earlier in his critique of the PBS book's section "In Search of Origins." Words and pictures were used so that a reader would draw a conclusion by inference that the written words did not actually state. This is what is done to school children when microevolutionary examples are provided as the mechanism of macroevolution.

That Microevolution Does Not Explain Macroevolution Is Old News to Evolutionary Biologists

It is a fundamental observation of humans that effects have causes. What are the supposed causes of macroevolution? In November 1980, a conference of some of the world's leading evolutionary biologists, billed as 'historic,' was held at the Chicago Field Museum of Natural History on the topic of 'macroevolution.' Reporting on the conference in the journal *Science* (Vol. 210 (4472):883–887, 1980.), Roger Lewin wrote: "The central question of the Chicago conference was whether the mechanisms underlying microevolution can be extrapolated to explain the phenomena of macroevolution. At the risk of doing violence to the positions of some of the people at the meeting, the answer can be given as a clear, No." Yet, examples of microevolution are still being used in textbooks to fool children into believing what all evolutionary biologists know is true: Microevolution does not explain the supposed macroevolution.

The Influence of Dawkins and Hawking

If as explained in the chapter on cosmic evolution, the materialistic models of cosmic origins are under attack in the 21st century by the theoretical physicists who publish in the professional, peer-reviewed technical journals, and since all such models depend on the contradiction, "causality without a cause," why do so many believe it?

If, as shown above in this chapter, evolutionary biology has no value to scientists producing goods and services in the medical and life sciences field and even biologists who believe in evolution know of no mechanism for macroevolution, why do so many believe it?

One explanation is the educational system's continuous use of axioms instead of explanations. When axioms are used, students are led to understand that the matter being considered is so well established as a fact that no explanation is to be expected. So no additional explanation is given. The observation by Jacques Monod, biochemist and winner of the 1965 Nobel Prize for Physiology or Medicine goes to the heart of the problem of belief without knowledge:

> Another curious aspect of the theory of evolution is that everybody thinks he understands it."

In the present era, considerable credit for belief in ideas that should be dismissed with "the Emperor has no clothes" goes to two best-selling books of the 1980s.

In his book 2021 *The Return of the God Hypothesis: Three Scientific Discoveries That Reveal The Mind Behind The Universe*, Stephen Meyer explained the impact that these two books made at Cambridge University when he was there earning his Ph. D. in the philosophy of science:

> During the late1980s, two important books gained enormous prominence there and around the world. In 1986. Oxford University biologist Richard Dawkins published *The Blind Watchmaker: Why the Evidence of Evolution Reveals a Universe Without Design*—a book that eventually sold three million copies.

Dawkin's title was a play on the theistic argument that if you found a watch on a beach you would assume the existence of a watchmaker. Meyer continued:

> A line from the first page succinctly captured his thesis: "Biology is the study of complicated things that *give the appearance* of having been designed for a purpose." Since, Dawkins argued, evolutionary theory explains this appearance as the product of the wholly undirected process of mutation and natural selection, it also eliminates the need to posit any role for a designing intelligence in the history of life. And that, he argued, "made it possible to be an intellectually fulfilled atheist."

> Then, in 1988, Stephen Hawking, at Cambridge, published *A Brief History of Time*. Whereas Dawkins took aim at the deign argument in biology, Hawking sought to undermine the cosmological argument for God's existence. Hawking's bestseller eclipsed even Dawkin's by eventually topping ten million copies sold worldwide.

On a personal note, Dawkin's book turned one of my Catholic nieces with two science degrees into an atheist in her 50s. Hawking's book created a lot of confusion in the mind of one of my sons (from which he recovered.)

Meyer went on to explain how those two books powerfully shaped public opinion:

> In Cambridge, Hawking's reputation as a physicist and his growing international celebrity hovered over almost all discussions of science and religion. If Stephen Hawking had explained the origin of the universe with a new law of quantum gravity, well, "What place, then, for a creator?" indeed. And, if Neo-Darwinism had shown that mutation and natural selection could explain away the appearance of design in life, as Dawkins had argued in his brilliantly clear prose, then life might well have resulted from a "blind watchmaker" (or "blind pitiless indifference," as he later put it) and nothing more.
>
> Dawkins and Hawking both either argued or implied, as Hawking later contended, that, "the simplest explanation is that there is no God." Consequently, their books encouraged the perception that science and theistic belief conflict.
>
> Those few theists that I met in the sciences, including a group in Britain called "Christians in Science" had adopted a defensive posture.

Meyer went on to explain how many subscribed to "compartmentalism" or "nonoverlapping magisteria." The model holds that science and religion describe entirely different realities. Others, according Meyer, subscribed to a closely related idea called "complementarity." Proponents of that view hold that science and religion may sometimes describe the same realities, however, they do so in complementary but ultimately incompatible or "noncommensurable" language. A great example of that is the way in which Bishop Robert Barron, the former chairman of the USCCB's Commission on Evangelization and Catechesis described the plain historical narrative of creation in the Book of Genesis. It is not history,

> it is "theology, mysticism, spirituality; a theological reflection on the origin of all things."

Meyer pointed out that

> Proponents of both views deny that science contradicts religious belief, but they do so by portraying science and religion as such totally distinct enterprises that their claims could not possibly intersect in any significant way.

That assumption, he maintains, insulates theists from scientific refutation of their belief in God but it also denies "the possibility that science could offer any support for theist belief."

Evolution is Secular Theology

Most Catholics shrug and say "So what!" because they don't understand that evolution is a dogma of a religion that hates Catholicism. In his book, *The Genesis of a Humanist Manifesto*, Edwin H. Wilson, one of the founders and preeminent leaders of the Humanist movement, explained how evolutionary cosmology and biological evolution undergird Humanism. Wilson wrote that "Humanism came of age in 1933 with the publication of *Humanist Manifesto I*." Wilson stated that its affirmations of faith regarding cosmology, biological and cultural evolution, human nature, epistemology, ethics, religion, self-fulfillment and the quest for freedom and social justice described precisely "the leading ideas and aspirations of its era."

That was no idle boast. Edwin Wilson correctly observed that *The Humanist Manifesto* reflected the reality that by 1933 "what was conceived by the convergence of freethought and religious liberalism at the end of the Nineteenth Century" had come to reign in the universities, if not yet in the local school houses.

From all that has gone before in this book, one ought to wonder why cosmic and biological evolution seem completely uncontroversial in American culture. Nobody or no institution of importance, not even the Catholic Church, questions it.

For one thing, there is no "push back" from the industrial and commercial engineering and scientific community because the theories are irrelevant to operational science. In the practical world that produces goods and services whether evolution is true or false, it doesn't matter.

The domain of evolutionary thought and discourse is the university and, by "trickle down," the K-12 schools. How did explanations for the origin of everything become the standard in education when even those who know the most about those explanations realize their shortcomings? Believers can demonstrate no mechanism for the things they say it has produced but that doesn't reduce their zeal for promoting it.

From the numerous examples given one can see that all evolutionary speculations qualify as "science" provided that they exclude God. Evolutionism fills the gap of "no God" because it answers for those who believe it answers "questions of ultimate concern" that are beyond science and formerly were considered religion and philosophy.

C.S. Lewis was not the first to notice this but he often remarked about it. For example, in a 1944 address to the Oxford University Socratic Club he said:

More disquieting still is Professor D. M. S. Watson's defense. "Evolution itself," he wrote, "is accepted by zoologists not because it has been observed to occur or... can be proved by logically coherent evidence to be true, but because the only alternative, special creation, is clearly incredible." Has it come to that? Does the whole vast structure of modern naturalism depend not on positive evidence but simply on an *a priori* metaphysical prejudice? Was it devised not to get in facts but to keep out God?

British philosopher Mary Midgley recognized long ago that
Evolution is the creation myth of our age. By telling us our origins it shapes our views of what we are. It influences not just our thoughts but also our actions in a way which goes far beyond its official function as a biological theory.

World-famous Yale University computer scientist David Gelernter created a sensation when he stated in *The Claremont Review of Books* May 2019, that Darwinism is no longer just a scientific theory but the basis of a worldview, and an emergency replacement religion for the many troubled souls who need one. https://www.claremont.org/download_pdf.php?file_name=1513G elernter.pdf

Believe Divine Revelation Instead of Fallible Men
Who are "the many troubled souls" for whom evolutionism is "an emergency replacement religion?" Stephen Hawking (d. 2018) was a theoretical physicist and cosmologist at Cambridge University and was a media-made celebrity. He conjured up new theories and it did not seem to matter how speculative his theories were. In 2018 celebrity astrophysicist and Hayden Planetarium director Neil deGrasse Tyson hosted "Star Talk" on

the National Geographic Cable Channel. Tyson believes we evolved from the stars. It is hilarious watching Tyson nodding and saying "uh huh" while pretending to understand Hawking's explanation of the universe's beginning.
/www.youtube.com/watch?v=FJ88kC2Nx8M

In a book Hawking co-authored, *The Grand Design,* published in 2010, one finds his opinion that

> It is not necessary to invoke God to light the blue touch paper and set the universe going. Instead, the laws of science alone can explain why the universe began. Our modern understanding of time suggests that it is just another dimension, like space. Thus, it doesn't have a beginning. Because there is a law such as gravity, the universe can and will create itself from nothing. Spontaneous creation is the reason there is something rather than nothing, why the universe exists, why we exist.

The First Dogma

In asserting that time had no beginning and the universe created itself from nothing, Hawking was preaching the first dogma of Humanism. One does not have to be a famous scientist to tell us that the universe created itself from nothing. Non-scientist Humanist philosophers, such as John Dewey, told the world the same thing in 1933 when they published *Humanist Manifesto I.* The Humanists described themselves as a new religion, that is, a religious movement meant to transcend and replace deity-based religions:

> While this age does owe a vast debt to the traditional religions, it is none the less obvious that any religion that can hope to be a synthesizing and dynamic force for today must be shaped for the needs of this age. To establish such a religion is a major necessity of the present. It is a

133

responsibility which rests upon this generation. We therefore affirm the following:

First: Religious humanists regard the universe as self-existing and not created.

Second: Humanism believes that man is a part of nature and that he has emerged as a result of a continuous process.

Third: Holding an organic view of life, humanists find that the traditional dualism of mind and body must be rejected.

In plain language, Humanists believe and teach others to believe, that cosmic and biological evolution produced the universe and its soulless inhabitants from eternally-existent inert matter. Of course, that is not capable of being proved but Humanists just assert it as an axiom, i.e., a statement or proposition which is regarded by Humanists as being established, accepted, or self-evidently true.

How Did That Result Come to Be?

How can it be that the theory of evolution, with no empirical evidence to support it, has become accepted as the scientific consensus and sixty-five percent of American adults believe it?" The short answer to that question is that people believe what they have been taught by the American education institutions such as schools and universities and are also affected by cultural influences. The long answer requires an explanation of how Humanist philosophy has dominated America since its founding and how Humanists have both converted and neutralized Christians. Dennis Q. McInerny, when he was Professor of Philosophy at Our Lady of Guadalupe Seminary, summarized that conversion process as follows:

> Over the course of the past century and a half, Western society has allowed itself to be convinced by something

which, from a strictly scientific point of view, is singularly unconvincing. I speak of the theory of evolution. But if this theory fails to make the grade as serious science, it has managed to succeed spectacularly as a philosophy, a comprehensive worldview, whose presence is pervasive and whose influence is as powerful as it is deleterious. Its invasion of our educational system is complete, and for decades now the nation's youth have been systematically indoctrinated to accept as an unquestionable "fact" what, in fact, is anything but.

The New Gospel

In *The Doctrines of Genesis 1-11* scientist-priest Victor Warkulwiz observed that "The doctrine of an ancient cosmos is asserted and proclaimed as a fact so often in scientific presentations, even when the context doesn't call for it, that it becomes obvious that a "gospel" is being preached. The name of that "gospel" is *Humanist Manifesto I* which has been the practical Creed of the American education industry even if many or most educators never heard of *Humanist Manifesto I* (1933).

Why Truth Matters, Why Genesis Matters

In the early chapters of *Genesis,* we find that the major doctrines of the Catholic faith have their origins: man and morality, free will, sin, the Fall, the Immaculate Conception, the Redeemer, the Godhead, sex, marriage, etc. *Genesis* explains why the world is in the state that it is, even though it was created in a state of perfection by an all-powerful, good, and loving God. If a person does not understand what *Genesis* is teaching then it is impossible to fully understand the central message of Christianity: the necessity of Redemption and faith in Jesus and the real hope that the Gospel provides. A re-interpretation of the plain reading of *Genesis* inevitably leads to attempts to alter the

135

traditional understanding of other biblical texts and pulling a host of Bible-based doctrines 'off the shelf.'

The choice is up to those priests and bishops on whom the laity depend. They can keep managing the decline and apostacy. They can keep teaching evolutionary biblical exegesis to the seminarians and produce another generation incapable of teaching creation doctrine. Alternatively, they could start promoting a creation catechesis that includes apologetics based on 21st century science. The organizations and their plentiful, often free, resources to revive catechesis exist. Many are listed in Appendix III.

Appendix I- Was Our Lady's Ancestor a Beast?

To even ask the question may seem blasphemous, but that Our Lady descended from an animal is the logical conclusion that Catholics who believe and promote the theory of evolution refuse to acknowledge.

Many well-meaning educators have sought to counter the alleged superiority of science over the Bible's *Genesis* creation narrative by embracing the "faux science" at the expense of the Bible to "interpret away" the conflict. Through a combination of scientific ignorance and dissent from the Magisterium about biblical inerrancy they are promoting cosmic and biological evolution as mainstream as long as one understands that "God did it."

The theory of evolution is that all humans descended from non-humans, that is, that there is biological continuity between animals and humans. That theory, promoted as a fact by the secular "scientific consensus," is the thesis of Charles Darwin's second most-famous book, *The Descent of Man, and Selection in Relation to Sex* first published in 1871. Darwin's second book applied to humans the evolutionary theory developed in his *On the Origin of Species by Means of Natural Selection, or the Preservation of Favored Races in the Struggle for Life,* published in 1859. According to a social survey published in 2019 by Pew Research, 87% of Catholics believe humans descended from animals, literally, from beasts. There is no way of escaping the conclusion that if humans descended from animals, so did Our Lady and for that matter, so did Our Lord.

Appendix II- Is the Pro-Homosexual Culture Connected to Belief in Evolution?

In the first chapter of St. Paul's epistle to the Romans, he explains the guilt of those who lie and suppress the truth about God. He explains what will happen to their culture. Surely when social research shows that 30% of Americans and half of the millennial generation does not believe in God, many persons have been actively and passively surprising the truth of our supernatural origins. They substitute the truth with stories of cosmic and biological evolution. The Christian religion has been replaced in many institutions by practical Humanism which is religious atheism. Among the practical consequences may be the cultural promotion of homosexualism and trans- genderism.

> [18] For the wrath of God is revealed from heaven against all ungodliness and wickedness of those who by their wickedness suppress the truth. [19] For what can be known about God is plain to them, because God has shown it to them. [20] Ever since the creation of the world his eternal power and divine nature, invisible though they are, have been understood and seen through the things he has made. So they are without excuse;

St. Paul described how God punishes the suppression of truth:

> [21] for though they knew God, they did not honor him as God or give thanks to him, but they became futile in their thinking, and their senseless minds were darkened. [22] Claiming to be wise, they became fools; [23] and they exchanged the glory of the immortal God for images resembling a mortal human being or birds or four-footed animals or reptiles.

Anthropologists have discovered that all people in all times have had a belief in some sort of higher power or god. Usually, in their ignorance, various nations have had gods such as contemporaries of the Israelites who worshiped Baal Moloch, conceived under the form of a calf or as a man with the head of a bull.

> [24] Therefore God gave them up in the lusts of their hearts to impurity, to the degrading of their bodies among themselves, [25] because they exchanged the truth about God for a lie and worshiped and served the creature rather than the Creator, who is blessed forever! Amen.

The principal pillars of Baalism were child sacrifice, sexual immorality (both heterosexual and homosexual) and pantheism (reverence of creation over the Creator). Adults would gather around the altar of Baal. Infants would then be burned alive as a sacrificial offering to the deity. Amid horrific screams and the stench of charred human flesh, congregants – men and women alike – would engage in bisexual orgies. The ritual of convenience was intended to produce economic prosperity by prompting Baal to bring rain for the fertility of "mother earth." Worshipping Baal meant sacrificing human life, never your own, just the innocent newly born, so you might have prosperity here on earth. [2]

In modern times the crimes against humanity, especially the unborn, arise from the same worldview of those in the "save the planet" cult who revere "mother earth" over the Creator. The breakdown in our culture which is manifested by the acceptance of "gay" and "trans" is, according to Scripture, a punishment for the denial of God the Creator. Sixty-five percent of American adults attribute their existence to materialistic cosmic and biological evolution with or without divine intervention. Belief in the Creator and His creation as revealed in *Genesis* is so low even in Catholic circles, according to Cardinal Ratzinger in 1995 "...the creation account is noticeably and completely absent from catechesis, preaching, and even theology. The creation narratives go unmentioned; it is asking too much to expect anyone to speak of them."

> [26] For this reason God gave them up to degrading passions. Their women exchanged natural intercourse for unnatural, [27] and in the same way also the men, giving up natural intercourse with women, were consumed with passion for one another. Men committed shameless acts with men and received in their own persons the due penalty for their error.

When we observe the things that ostensibly well-educated people in our leading institutions say and do in complete sincerity but which to us seems to be stupid, we wonder what is wrong with them. Most likely they are practical atheists "Claiming to be wise, they became fools."

> [28] And since they did not see fit to acknowledge God, God gave them up to a debased mind and to things that should not be done. [29] They were filled with every kind of wickedness, evil, covetousness, malice. Full of envy, murder, strife, deceit, craftiness, they are gossips, [30] slanderers, God-haters, insolent, haughty, boastful, inventors of evil, rebellious toward parents, [31] foolish, faithless, heartless, ruthless. [32] They know God's decree, that those who practice such things deserve to die—yet they not only do them but even applaud others who practice them.

The description of the vices into which practical Humanists have fallen pretty much describes the political and cultural class that dominates us. Verse 32 applies also to the "straight" people who applaud the activity of the perverse by applauding "gay marriage" and the Gay Pride movement.

Appendix III-Science and Catholicism Resources

See scienceandcatholicism.org for a highly-discounted bundle of books from the Institute for Science and Catholicism (ISC)

The Evolution of Catholic Unbelief (ISC, 2019) explains the role of schools in peeling away young Catholics and how priests contribute to the problem by teaching evolution and trying to "baptize" it by saying that "God did it." This short book shows how Catholics are miseducated out of their faith by Catholic teachers of bogus science who ignore Sacred Tradition in favor of Humanist speculation. It challenges Catholic lay intellectuals to inform themselves and teach the truth. A "give away" book to acquaint others with the evolution menace.

Creation, Evolution, and Catholicism: A Discussion for Those Who Believe (ISC, updated 2023) is a comprehensive exposition of the science, philosophy, history, and theology involved. It is an expanded version of this present book to include analysis of Church teaching since the late 19th century and details of the growth of Humanism's cultural control of the U. S.

Intellectual Combat: Resistance to Religious Atheism (ISC, 2021) discusses the concept of "religious atheism," which is also known as Humanism. Humanism is an ideology that promotes "good without God" and has a long history dating back to the 19th century. Many atheists adopt Humanism, which has a common core of beliefs and a worldview that coincides with Humanism's creed. The book shows that once society rejects God, it can lead to frightening social, political, and spiritual consequences.

Darwin's Doubt: The Explosive Origin of Animal Life and the Case for Intelligent Design by Stephen C. Meyer. This is a 2013 *NYT* Bestseller. It is very readable for the ordinary non-scientist.

Darwin's House of Cards: A Journalist's Odyssey through the Darwin Debates (2017) by Tom Bethell is a masterpiece of science, history, and philosophy by a non-scientist.

Foresight: How the Chemistry of Life Reveals Planning and Purpose (2019) by Marcos Eberlin a Brazilian with over a 1000 published scientific articles. His book is chock full of amazing descriptions such as human reproduction, migratory bird navigation, bacteria, bugs and carnivorous plants that demonstrate "foresight" (meaning intelligent design).

Spacecraft Earth: A Guide for Passengers (2017) by Dr. Henry Richter debunks evolutionary cosmology by explaining how rare the Earth is. Easy reading for the non-scientist.

Zombie Science (2017) by Jonathan Wells. Easy read for the non-scientist. Debunks dead science still taught in schools.

Aquinas and Evolution (2017) by Michael Chaberek. O.P. explains why St. Thomas's teaching on the origin of species is incompatible with evolutionary theory. Refutes miseducated Dominicans promoting evolution as "Thomistic."

Kolbe Center for the Study of Creation (online at kolbecenter.org) has a vast amount of free reading and great books for sale. This is the website for authentic Catholic creation theology and natural science. The Kolbe Center will provide a free seminar to any group or institution. Follow on Facebook.

The Institute for Creation Research (online at icr.org) is a premier creation-supporting science resource. In addition to so much free information online, ICR sells books and DVDs suitable for all ages. Sign up online for a free monthly magazine called *Acts & Facts*, full of science that is written for non-scientists.

Creation Ministries International (online at creation.com) Subscribe to CMI's free daily email science articles and get a creation science education day by day. This is a super resource that also furnishes free creation science video.

The Discovery Institute's Center for Science and Culture (online at discovery.org/id/) is a comprehensive resource offering much free evidence from physics, astronomy, chemistry, biology, and related fields that nature is the product of intelligent design rather than blind, unguided processes. Subscribe and get a free email called Nota Bene. Look at www.evolutionnews.org.

The Creation Research Society is a professional membership organization of scientists and laypersons committed to scientific special creation and a young earth. They publish a great quarterly of scientific importance. creationresearch.org/

The Biblical Science Institute (biblescienceinstitute.com) Sign up for free newsletter.

Center for Scientific Creation (online at creationscience.com/) Comprehensive info on the Flood and the earth's geology.

Daylight Origins Society-Creation science in the UK and Ireland www.daylightorigins.com

****

Institute for Science and Catholicism (ISC) We mail copies of this book to priests, seminarians, and others. Will you support this evangelization effort with a tax-deductible donation to ISC by using the "donate" button on our website's home page? Scienceandcatholicism.org

Made in the USA
Middletown, DE
23 September 2023

39099083R00086